THE HUNGER GAMES

Suzanne Collins

SPARK PUBLISHING

Spark Publishing
A Division of Barnes & Noble
120 Fifth Avenue
New York, NY 10011
www.sparknotes.com

ISBN: 978-1-4114-7098-9

Please submit changes or report errors to www.sparknotes.com/errors.

Printed in Canada

10 9 8 7 6 5 4 3 2 1

Contents

Context

Growing up, Suzanne Collins was a military brat. Her father was a career airman in the United States Air Force. As a result, Collins and her siblings—two older sisters and an older brother—moved around frequently, spending time in numerous locations in the eastern United States as well as in Europe. The military, in fact, played a leading role in the family's history. Collins's grandfather had served in World War I, her uncle served in World War II, and the year Collins turned six, her father left to serve his own tour in the Vietnam War. War, consequently, was a part of life for Collins, something very real and not just an abstract idea. While her father was gone, she would sometimes see video footage of the war zone on the news, and she recognized that her father was there fighting.

Though her father returned after a year, Collins's connection to war didn't end. In addition to being a soldier, Collins's father was also a military historian and a doctor of political science. That knowledge and his experiences serving in the Air Force and fighting in Vietnam had a profound effect on his relationship with his children, and he made sure they learned about war. While other girls' fathers were telling them fairytales, Collins's father educated his children about military history. When the family was moved to Brussels, Belgium, for instance, her father educated her about the region's violent past and took her on tours of the country's historic battlefields.

Eventually, Collins attended Indiana University. There, she met the man who would later become her husband, Cap Pryor. At 25, she began an M.F.A. program at New York University where she specialized in playwriting, and after graduation, worked for about a year before landing her first television-writing job on the show "Hi Honey, I'm Home!" Since then, Collins has been on the writing staff of several shows, including the Emmy-nominated "Clarissa Explains It All." She and her family, now including two children, left New York for Connecticut. Collins began work on her first series of books for children, *The Underland Chronicles*. The series was another success for Collins, making the *New York Times* best-seller list. Collins was 41 when the first book in the series, *Gregor the Overlander*, was published.

One night, Collins was watching television, flipping back and forth between coverage of the wars in Iraq and Afghanistan and a reality-TV show. That's when Collins had the idea that would ultimately turn into *The Hunger Games*. A longtime fan of Greek and Roman mythology, Collins borrowed a great deal from those sources to give the story its shape. One notable contribution came from the story of Theseus and the Minotaur, in which the Cretan king Minos demanded that seven maidens and seven youths be sent as a tribute every nine years. He gave these tributes to the Minotaur, who would consume them. Collins also borrowed from Ancient Roman history. The gladiatorial games were updated and turned into a televised competition, and Collins took the name of her fictional dystopia from the Latin phrase *panem et circenses* (bread and circuses). While Collins finished her often dark and violent book, she continued to write for television, working on the markedly less violent show "Wow! Wow! Wubbzy!"

The Hunger Games was published in September 2008 and quickly found critical success with reviewers and other authors, including Stephen King, praising the book. Among the features that received the most attention were the plotting and pace. Collins has attributed her skill in these areas to her background as a playwright and her time spent working in television, where there is little downtime allowed and character development has to occur simultaneously with the storyline constantly moving forward. The book also rose to the top of the *New York Times* bestseller list and subsequently spent more than three consecutive years on the list. The other books in the trilogy, published over the next two years, followed the same pattern, all becoming huge commercial successes. Then, in March 2012, *The Hunger Games* movie was released. It had the third-highest opening weekend in history, and the highest opening weekend ever for a movie that was not a sequel. There are now more than 18 million copies of *The Hunger Games* in print, and with the trilogy now available in fifty languages, the books have genuinely become a worldwide phenomenon.

PLOT OVERVIEW

Katniss Everdeen wakes up on the day of the reaping, when the tributes are chosen who will take part in the Hunger Games. Her mother and little sister, Prim, sleep nearby. Her father died in a mine explosion years earlier. She goes hunting in the woods outside her district, District 12, with Gale, her best friend. That night, at the reaping ceremony, the mayor gives a speech describing how the governments of North America collapsed and the country of Panem rose up in their place. A war ensued between the Capitol and the districts. The Capitol won, and as a reminder of their defeat, the Capitol holds the Hunger Games every year. The mayor then introduces Haymitch Abernathy, District 12's only living Hunger-Games winner, who is so drunk he ends up falling in his own vomit.

The district's female tribute is chosen, and to Katniss's horror, it's Prim. Katniss volunteers immediately to take Prim's place. Then the male tribute is selected. It's Peeta Mellark, and Katniss remembers that Peeta gave her bread from his family's bakery years earlier, while she was searching for food for her family in the garbage bins behind the town shops. Katniss credits him with saving her that day. Katniss and Peeta say good-bye to their friends and families and board a train for the Capitol. During the trip, she and Peeta convince Haymitch, their mentor in the Games and the person responsible for getting them gifts from sponsors, to take his duties seriously.

Once there, Katniss meets with her stylist, Cinna, who is designing her dress for the opening ceremony. At the ceremony, Katniss and Peeta wear simple black outfits lit with synthetic flames. The outfits are a huge hit with the audience and make Katniss and Peeta stand out among the tributes. The next day, Katniss and Peeta attend group training, and the tributes from rich districts who have trained for the Games their whole lives, called Career Tributes, show off their skills. Later, the tributes are interviewed by Caesar Flickerman, a television host. In his interview, Peeta reveals that he's had a crush on Katniss for several years.

Finally the time comes. From a small underground room, Katniss is lifted into the arena and the Games officially begin. All the tributes are there, and in front of her is the Cornucopia, which houses an abundance of supplies. Rather than fight, she runs away as Haymitch advised. She hikes all day before making camp. After dark, someone starts a fire nearby, and it isn't long before a pack of Career Tributes arrives and kills the person. To Katniss's shock, Peeta is with them. The next day Katniss goes in search of water. She walks for hours and collapses from exhaustion, but ultimately she finds a stream. She's awakened during the night by a wall of fire moving in her direction, and as she runs away, one of the numerous fireballs falling around her grazes her leg, injuring it.

That night, while she hides in a tree from the pack of Careers below, she notices a young girl named Rue from District 11 in a nearby tree. Rue points out a nest of tracker jackers, wasps engineered by the Capitol to be lethal, over Katniss's head, and Katniss cuts the branch holding the nest, dropping it onto the Careers. Two of them die from the stings and the rest scatter. Katniss is stung a few times as well, but as she's running away, she remembers that one of the girls who died had a bow and arrows, the weapons she's become proficient with from hunting. She runs back to retrieve them, and Peeta happens to arrive as she's grabbing the bow. He yells at Katniss to run just as Cato, a very large and dangerous Career from District 2, shows up. Peeta stops him so Katniss can escape, and she passes out in a ditch shortly after.

Katniss encounters Rue again, and the two quickly form a bond. They are able to get food hunting and foraging, and Katniss realizes that the Careers will have difficulty surviving without the supplies at the Cornucopia, so she and Rue devise a plan. While Rue lights decoy fires, Katniss sneaks up to the Cornucopia. The supplies are in a pyramid away from the main camp, and after the Careers leave to investigate the fires, Katniss manages to blow up the supplies by cutting open a bag of apples with her arrows. The falling apples trigger the mines set to protect the pyramid. When Katniss doesn't find Rue at their meeting spot, she goes looking for her and finds her just as another tribute stabs her with a spear. Katniss kills the other tribute, and when Rue dies, Katniss covers her body in flowers.

Katniss is depressed all the next day, until an announcement is made that there has been a rule change: Now, two tributes from the same district can be declared winners. Katniss goes looking for Peeta. It takes her a day, but finally she finds him. He's severely injured from his fight with Cato and can barely walk, but Katniss helps him to a cave where they'll be hidden. Thinking Peeta may die, Katniss impulsively kisses him. A moment later she hears a noise outside and finds a pot of broth sent from Haymitch. She realizes that Haymitch will reward her for playing up the romance with Peeta. The next morning Katniss sees that Peeta's leg is badly infected and he'll die without treatment. Another announcement is made, this time saying each tribute will find a crucial item at the Cornucopia. Katniss knows that means medicine for Peeta's leg, but Peeta thinks it's too dangerous and doesn't want Katniss to go. Using a sleep syrup sent from Haymitch, Katniss knocks him out.

At the Cornucopia, Katniss tries to run and grab the item marked for District 12, but she gets into a fight with a female tribute. The tribute is about to kill her when Thresh, the male tribute from District 11 who came to the Games with Rue, kills the girl instead. He spares Katniss because of the way she treated Rue, and Katniss makes it back to the cave. She injects Peeta with the medicine just before he passes out. They stay there for a few days while it rains nonstop outside, and in this time the romance between Katniss and Peeta progresses. When the rain lets up, Peeta and Katniss need to find food. Katniss leaves Peeta in charge of foraging while she goes to hunt. She comes back hours later and finds a small pile of poisonous berries Peeta collected thinking they were safe. They discover the body of a tribute whom Katniss nicknamed Foxface, and Katniss realizes she died from eating the berries. At this point Cato, who has killed Thresh, is the only tribute left, and Katniss decides to keep some berries in case they can trick Cato into eating them. Eventually the streams and ponds dry up, and they know the only source of water left is the lake near the Cornucopia. Without any other choice, they start walking to the lake.

By the lake, Cato comes suddenly barreling toward them. Unexpectedly, however, he runs straight by them. Katniss realizes there are strange creatures chasing him, and they all run to the Cornucopia and climb up. The creatures are mutant wolves engineered by the Capitol, and Katniss realizes they are actually the dead tributes, who have been turned into these monsters. Taking advantage of the situation, Cato attacks Peeta, but Katniss and Peeta manage to push Cato over the edge. The creatures overpower him, but because of the body armor he's wearing he remains alive for hours, until, out of pity, Katniss shoots him. Just as Katniss and Peeta think they've won, another announcement is made that there can only be one winner. Neither Katniss nor Peeta will kill the other, so Katniss takes out the poisonous berries. Just as she and Peeta pop them in their mouths, the announcer shouts for them to stop and declares them both winners.

They go back to the Training Center, and Katniss is kept alone for days while she recuperates. When she is let out, Haymitch warns her that she's in danger. The Capitol viewed her stunt with the berries as an act of defiance, so she has to convince everyone that she was desperate at the thought of losing Peeta and was not being rebellious; otherwise, even her family could be at risk. In their final interview, she's reunited with Peeta, who lost his leg and now has a prosthesis. Afterward, when Haymitch tells her she did great, Peeta wonders what he means, and Katniss explains everything, including the romance strategy during the Games. Peeta is angry and hurt, but as they arrive back in District 12, they hold hands one more time to greet the crowd and cameras.

Character List

Katniss Everdeen the protagonist and female tribute of District 12. She is an excellent hunter and tremendously resourceful.

Peeta Mellark the boy tribute of District 12 and the son of a baker. He is kind and loyal, and he becomes Katniss's love interest and main ally during the Hunger Games.

Haymitch Abernathy Katniss and Peeta's trainer. He is a drunk and one of only two people from District 12 to have won the Hunger Games (and the only one still living).

Effie Trinket the escort of the tributes from District 12. She is very concerned with appearances and her own career.

Gale Katniss's friend and hunting partner. Gale is probably the person closest to Katniss, and he is the only one with whom she can ever fully relax and be herself.

Prim Everdeen Katniss's little sister. She is small and gentle, and Katniss volunteers in her place when her name is drawn in the reaping.

Mother (Everdeen) Katniss's mother. After her husband died, she essentially stopped caring for Katniss and Prim, forcing Katniss to become the family's primary provider.

Cinna Katniss's main stylist. He becomes Katniss's friend over the course of the story and counsels Katniss to be herself.

Madge Undersee the mayor's daughter and the only person Katniss is friendly with at school. She gives Katniss the mockingjay pin.

Mayor Undersee the mayor of District 12

Venia the person who waxes Katniss before she sees Cinna, her stylist

Cato the male tribute from District 2. He is a career tribute, meaning he has trained for the Hunger Games his entire life, and he is large, short-tempered, and a fierce fighter.

Rue the female tribute from District 11. Katniss and Rue become allies during the Games.

Foxface a female tribute in the Hunger Games characterized by her wiliness and intelligence. She dies by eating poisonous berries collected by Peeta.

Thresh the male tribute from District 11. He shows mercy toward Katniss because of the way Katniss treated Rue.

Glimmer the female tribute from District 1. She dies when Katniss drops a tracker jacker nest on her and some other tributes.

Clove the female tribute from District 2. She actually defeats Katniss in a fight and nearly kills her, but Thresh intervenes and saves Katniss's life.

Caesar Flickerman the ostentatious television host who interviews Katniss and Peeta before and after the Games

Claudius Templesmith the announcer during the Hunger Games

President Snow the president of Panem

Analysis of Major Characters

Katniss Everdeen

The protagonist of the novel and its narrator, Katniss Everdeen is a strong, resourceful sixteen-year-old who is far more mature than her age would suggest. Katniss is the main provider in her family, which consists of herself, her mother, and her younger sister, Prim. Katniss is fiercely protective of her younger sister, and she volunteers to take Prim's place in the Hunger Games to protect her. In fact, Katniss is more responsible than anyone else for her family's well-being. Notably, she is responsible for feeding her family, which she does by hunting and foraging, skills she learned from her father before his death in a mine explosion years earlier. Hunting, however, is illegal and punishable by death. Katniss does it anyway, indicating a rebellious streak. Moreover, what she catches or collects that her family doesn't need to eat, she sells in the district's black market, again implying a disregard for rules.

This disregard, however, developed out of necessity rather than an inherent defiance. After Katniss's father died, her mother sank into a depression, leaving Katniss to take care of the family despite her young age. Katniss realized that, without her hunting, her family wouldn't have enough to eat, a serious problem in District 12, where starvation is common. As a result of these conditions, Katniss has grown into a tough, unsentimental, and practical young woman. Ironically, the hardships she faced as a result of her impoverished upbringing wind up working to her advantage once she's in the arena. The skills and qualities she developed to cope with the everyday challenges of being poor—including her ability to hunt, her toughness, and her resourcefulness—turn out to be what keep her alive through the Games.

During the weeks when the Games occur, Katniss's character does not fundamentally change. What changes are her circumstances, and most of the novel watches her deal with the situations she encounters. She does not seek attention once she becomes a celebrity and begins doing television interviews. Rather, she always tries to figure out how to get through the interviews so she can go back to her life. The Hunger Games, similarly, do not turn her into an unfeeling killer, and the only times she kills she does so out of necessity, and to some degree in Cato's case, pity. That her sense of compassion remains intact is clear in the way she treats Rue. Furthermore, before the Games, she has little interest in boys and is instead focused on her responsibilities, and though she develops feelings for Peeta and becomes aware of feelings for Gale during the Games, romance remains a peripheral interest for her at the end of the novel. This lack of change, however, can be seen as a victory for Katniss. She maintains her sense of identity and integrity, just as Peeta at one point says he would like to, despite the horrible ordeals she faces in the Games.

PEETA MELLARK

The male tribute from District 12, Peeta is in love with Katniss and becomes her main ally and romantic interest during the Games. Peeta is best characterized by his love for Katniss and willingness to sacrifice himself for her. Katniss's first memory of him, for instance, is from an incident years before the Games in which Peeta willingly risked a beating to help her. Katniss was starving and searching for food behind Peeta's family's bakery, and Peeta apparently burned two loaves of bread deliberately so the bakery couldn't use them, then gave those loaves to Katniss. Peeta's mother hit him for burning the bread, and Katniss believes Peeta must have known he would be punished for it. During the Games, he is similarly selfless when he saves Katniss after she comes back to retrieve the bow and finds herself suddenly stunned by the tracker jacker stings. To allow Katniss to escape, Peeta fights Cato, the most deadly of the other tributes, and suffers a serious injury as a result.

Though we have a limited perspective of Peeta since we only seen him through Katniss's eyes, he comes across as thoughtful, artistic, and genuinely kind. We learn that he's a gifted visual artist, capable of creating beautiful designs in frosting for the cakes at his family's bakery and mimicking patterns of light and shade when he camouflages himself. When Haymitch falls in his own vomit, it is Peeta who volunteers to clean him up. Katniss wonders what his motive is in volunteering for this task, then realizes that Peeta is just being nice. In one particularly memorable scene before the Games occur, Peeta confesses to Katniss that his only hope for the Games is to retain his identity and not to be made into a monster by his circumstances. The incident reveals Peeta to be a good and introspective person who prides his dignity and decency perhaps above all else. (It is never made clear whether he would sacrifice that for Katniss as well.)

HAYMITCH ABERNATHY

As District 12's only surviving winner of the Hunger Games, Haymitch acts as Katniss and Peeta's coach throughout the Games. Though he is drunk most, in fact nearly all, of the time, he proves a cunning adviser to the young tributes. It is never explicitly said in the novel, but it appears to be Haymitch who devises the strategy of playing up the romance between Katniss and Peeta, a move that ultimately allows both of them to survive the Games even though traditionally only one winner has been allowed. Haymitch also finds a way of communicating with Katniss during the Games through the gifts he sends her, essentially coaching her on how she should behave to get more sponsors. Albeit in a very limited way, he also acts as somewhat of a father figure to Katniss, who lost her father years earlier. While Haymitch is often indelicate and manipulative, frequently using Peeta and his feelings for Katniss to get the results he wants, he is undeniably effective. When Katniss and Peeta wonder how he won the Hunger Games, Peeta suspects he must have outsmarted the other tributes.

Themes, Motifs & Symbols

Themes

The inequality between rich and poor

In Panem, wealth is heavily concentrated in the hands of the rich, particularly those people living in the Capitol and certain of the districts, and the result is a huge disparity between their lives and the lives of the poor. This disparity reveals itself in numerous ways throughout the novel, notably in the area of food. In the poor districts, many of the residents do not have enough to eat. Katniss notes that starvation is common in District 12, and she has to hunt illegally in the woods beyond the district's borders to feed her family. The novel suggests that most of the district's residents are not able to hunt or don't know how to, meaning that even given the little Katniss's family has, it is still more than many of the other families in her district have. Furthermore, all but the most basic foods are luxuries. Katniss later learns that Peeta's family, which owns a bakery and is thus one of the more well-off in the district, can't afford most of the food they bake and eat mostly the stale leftovers that nobody buys. In contrast, when Katniss arrives in the Capitol, she is awed by the lavish feasts and elaborately prepared dishes. The food is rich and abundant, and Katniss, for the first time, tries hot chocolate.

Perhaps the best example of the inequality between rich and poor can be seen in the tessera system and the way the tributes are selected for the Games. In theory, the lottery by which tributes are chosen, called the reaping, is random and anyone can be picked. But in reality, the poor are much more likely than the rich to end up as tributes. In exchange for extra rations of grain and oil, called tesserae, those children eligible for the Hunger Games must enter their names into the reaping additional times. Most children of poor families have to take tesserae to survive, so the children of poor families have more entries in the reaping than children of wealthy families who need no tesserae. They're more likely to be picked as a result. Moreover, the rich who do become tributes tend to have an additional advantage, because they are often trained to take part in the Games and volunteer to do so. These trained tributes, whom Katniss refers to as Career Tributes, are generally bigger, stronger, and better prepared for the tribulations of the Hunger Games than those poor tributes selected by chance. Consequently, a rich tribute is more likely to win. For these rich tributes, it is an honor to compete in the Games, while for the poor tributes it is essentially a death sentence.

SUFFERING AS ENTERTAINMENT

The Hunger Games presents the tributes' suffering as mass entertainment, and the more the tributes suffer, ideally in battle with one another, the more entertaining the Games become. The main draw of the Games for viewers is its voyeurism, in this case watching the tributes, who are of course children, fighting and dying. Katniss at various points talks about past Games and what made them successful or unsuccessful, and the recurring motif is that the viewers want to see the tributes battling one another but not dying too quickly (because then the entertainment is over). The principle is best exemplified in Cato's slow death at the end of the novel. Once the muttations have defeated Cato, they don't kill him immediately, and Katniss realizes that the Gamemakers want Cato to remain alive because it creates an exceedingly gruesome spectacle. It is the finale of the Games, and so they want to deliver prolonged suffering the audience at home won't be able to turn away from. The suffering, however, doesn't have to be purely physical. It can be psychological as well. Katniss and Peeta's romance, for instance, is the subject of so much fascination because it is presumed to be doomed. They become the "star-crossed lovers," meaning ill-fated, and that promise of suffering adds drama and makes them fun to watch.

In essence, the Games are the equivalent of a televised sporting event in which several participants compete to win. Katniss even refers to the tributes as "players" sometimes when talking about the Games of past years. Most of the players, however, are unwilling, and winning entails outliving the other tributes, mostly by fighting and killing them. In both these ways the Hunger Games recall the gladiatorial games of ancient Rome (notably, the gladiatorial games were one of the most popular forms of entertainment of their time), in which armed competitors, some voluntarily and others not, would fight to the death. That the Games are televised and discussed incessantly in Panem's media also, of course, recalls today's reality television, and the novel consequently draws a parallel between the gladiatorial games and reality TV. This parallel suggests that reality television, though perhaps not quite as barbarous as the gladiatorial games, still offers up real life as entertainment, and in doing so it turns real people into commodities. Their value is determined by how much entertainment they provide, and as such they lose their identities as people. Reality television, the novel suggests, is a form of objectification.

THE IMPORTANCE OF APPEARANCES

Throughout the novel, Katniss and her team use her external appearance, including what she says and how she behaves, to control how other people perceive her. At the reaping ceremony, for instance, she won't allow herself to cry in front of the cameras because she doesn't want to give the impression of being weak (and therefore an easy target). Moreover, at the opening ceremony of the Games, the novel emphasizes how important appearances are by focusing a great deal on Katniss's preparations. The main feature of this focus is the dress Cinna creates for her. It is covered in synthetic flames, earning Katniss the epithet "the girl who was on fire," and it makes Katniss stand out among the tributes. Drawing attention is more than just vanity in the Games. The tributes that are most memorable tend to attract sponsors, who can provide gifts that may prove critical during the Games. Katniss hides her tears during the Games for a similar reason, as self-pitying tributes are unattractive to sponsors. A tribute's appearance and behavior can therefore serve as a significant part of their survival strategy.

Perhaps the most notable part of Katniss's strategy involves her romance with Peeta. This romance is not entirely genuine on Katniss's end. She cares about Peeta and develops a romantic interest in him, but her feelings don't have nearly the same intensity as his, and she always remains ambivalent about him. For the cameras, however, Katniss plays up her feelings for Peeta and works to convince the viewers, and especially the Capitol, that she's deeply in love with him. The act is one Haymitch devised for strategic reasons: Katniss and Peeta's love story elicits more gifts from sponsors than if they were simply friends, and it seems even to influence the Capitol's decision to allow two tributes to be declared winners rather than the customary one. Consequently, the act Katniss puts on has a significant effect on both her survival and Peeta's. Through these events, the novel suggests that what cameras show, on reality television for instance, is not necessarily reality, and that appearances are just as consequential as the truth.

MOTIFS

FIRE

Fire plays different roles throughout the story, but most often it represents Katniss. Notably, fire is the element that gives the various outfits Cinna designs for Katniss their character. Her first dress, for example, is covered in synthetic flames, while later outfits use fire more subtly but still maintain it as a motif. Katniss's fire dress earns her the epithet "the girl who was on fire," and this title comes to pertain to more than just her dress. After Katniss's surprisingly high training score is announced, Haymitch explains that they must have liked her "heat." Cinna calls her "the girl who was on fire" again, this time using "fire" to refer to Katniss's spirit and temperament. During the Games, the phrase takes on a literal meaning after Katniss is struck in the leg by a fireball and thinks the Gamemakers must be laughing at "the girl who was on fire."

DEFIANCE

The novel is full of acts of defiance against the Capitol despite the Capitol's authoritarian control over the people of Panem. Katniss and Gale's illegal hunting is an act of defiance, since they're willfully violating the Capitol's rules. The same can be said for the existence of the Hob, the bustling black market of District 12. The gesture of respect the residents of District 12 offer Katniss after she volunteers as tribute is similarly a form of defiance in that it contradicts the behavior the Capitol wants and expects to see. The mockingjay, which appears throughout the novel, represents defiance in that it recalls the Capitol's failures, and Peeta essentially hopes to defy the Capitol and Gamemakers when he tells Katniss he wants to retain his identity and show them he's not just a part of their Games. The most significant acts of defiance come from Katniss, however. Decorating Rue's body after her death directly violates the spirit of the Hunger Games, which demand that tributes show no mercy for one another, and Katniss's idea to threaten suicide with the berries shows that she and Peeta will not accept the Gamemakers' rules.

HUNTING

Hunting reappears numerous times in the story, but it takes on vastly different connotations depending on the circumstances. Katniss, we learn at the very beginning of the book, is a hunter, and she feeds her family primarily with what she can catch or kill in the woods outside District 12. In fact, she spends most of her day hunting, typically with her friend, Gale, and consequently it appears in one form or another in many of her stories about life before the Hunger Games. For instance, most of her stories about her father revolve around hunting. She also met Gale while hunting, and one of her favorite stories, the one she tells Peeta about how she managed to get a goat for Prim, begins with hunting. Hunting also allows her to stay alive during the Games when there is no other food to be found. In these circumstances, hunting is always a positive experience for Katniss.

In the context of the Hunger Games, however, hunting takes on a very different meaning. When Katniss talks to Gale before she leaves for the Training Center, he wonders if hunting a human will be any different from hunting an animal. As Katniss discovers, it is substantially different, and despite her experience killing animals for food, killing a person in a competition is emotionally traumatizing for her. Moreover, Peeta often refers to the Career Tributes as "hunting" when they're searching for other tributes to kill. Though the act of hunting remains essentially the same in the arena, the connotation shifts from a positive one for Katniss to an entirely negative one.

Symbols

Mockingjays

The mockingjay represents defiance in the novel, with the bird's symbolism deriving initially from its origins. The mockingjay, we learn, came about as a result of a failed project by the Capitol to spy on the rebellious districts, and since then the bird has served as a reminder of this failure and the districts' recalcitrance—Katniss describes them as "something of a slap in the face to the Capitol." The mockingjay pin Madge gives to Katniss is at first an emblem of that resistance. Later in the novel, however, the birds come to symbolize a different sort of defiance. Mockingjays become a link between Katniss and Rue, with the two using the birds to communicate. When Rue dies, Katniss decorates her body with flowers as a means of memorializing Rue, but also to defy the Capitol. When Katniss later sees mockingjays, they remind her of Rue, and that memory inevitably stirs her hatred of the Capitol and her wish to rebel and take revenge, against it. The mockingjay consequently takes on an additional layer of symbolism, representing not only a general rebellion against the Capitol, but also Katniss's specific spirit of defiance.

PANEM

Panem is the country in which *The Hunger Games* takes place, and it symbolizes a dystopian United States. The word *panem* is Latin for "bread," and given the similarity of the Hunger Games to the gladiatorial games of Ancient Rome, it recalls *panem et circenses*, or "bread and circuses." The phrase refers to the Roman Caesars' strategy of quelling public discontent by providing the people with plenty of food and entertainment. The entertainment, of course, was largely provided by gladiatorial games. In the novel, these gladiatorial games are blended with reality television to create the Hunger Games. Setting Panem in the location of the present-day United States, and retaining parts of U.S. culture like the mining industry of Appalachia that we see in District 12, draws a link between the two. But the metaphor gets more complicated because of the influences of Ancient Rome on Panem. The result is a metaphor that uses Panem to draw connections between Ancient Rome and the modern United States, suggesting that the modern United States has something like its own *panem et circenses* strategy in place, with reality television taking on the role of the gladiatorial games.

The metaphor offered by Panem, however, does not align perfectly with Ancient Rome's *panem et circenses* formula. For one, that formula is designed to keep the people content, but the people of Panem are decidedly not content, at least not in the poor districts. In fact, the Hunger Games, unlike the gladiatorial games which appeased the masses, play a significant role in their dissatisfaction. The Games were created as a reminder to the districts of their powerlessness after their uprising against the Capitol ended in defeat, and it is the children of the districts who are drafted involuntarily into the Games to be killed. Second, a key element of the *panem et circenses* strategy missing from Panem is the bread. Most of the people in the districts are severely underfed, and again this is a cause of much of the people's discontent. It leads directly to various forms of rebellion, such as Katniss's illegal hunting and the existence of a large black market in District 12. Rather than being a comment on the fictional Panem, it instead comments on the present-day United States in the ways described above, thus offering a valuable criticism of modern culture in the U.S.

Katniss's dresses

The dresses Cinna designs for Katniss not only give Katniss her epithet, "the girl who was on fire," but also come to symbolize her spirit. Cinna designs the first dress to reflect the main industry of Katniss's home district, coal mining. Since coal's purpose is to burn, Cinna creates a dress that would be lit with synthetic flames. This dress begins the association between Katniss and fire while also giving Katniss her epithet. That epithet comes to describe Katniss generally, however, and not just how she appears in Cinna's designs. Haymitch, for instance, explains Katniss's high training score by saying the judges must have liked her temper and her "heat." (Katniss also thinks the Gamemakers may have targeted her with fireballs in the arena as a reference to "the girl who was on fire.") The dresses, notably the first one for the opening ceremony but also the more subdued versions Cinna creates for Katniss's interviews, serve as outward, nearly literal representations of Katniss's inner "fire."

Summary & Analysis

Chapters 1–3

Summary: Chapter 1

Katniss Everdeen, who tells her story in the first person, wakes up. It is the day of the reaping. She sees her little sister, Prim (short for Primrose), asleep in bed with their mother across the room. Katniss puts on her clothes to go hunting. The area where she and her family live is called the Seam, and it's part of District 12. They are at the edge of the district, which is enclosed by a high fence, and Katniss often crawls under the fence and enters the woods outside, where she forages and hunts. Her father taught her these skills before his death in a mine explosion when she was eleven years old, and she uses a bow he made. Though trespassing in the woods and poaching are illegal, nobody pays attention, and Katniss even sells meat to the Peacekeepers who are supposed to enforce the laws. Most people in the district, she explains, don't have enough food.

She meets her friend Gale in the woods. They discuss running away, but both are the caretakers of their families. They catch some fish, then stop by the district's black market, called the Hob, to trade for bread and salt. They go to the mayor's house to sell strawberries they collected and talk to the mayor's daughter, Madge, whom Katniss is friendly with at school. Madge is dressed for the reaping in case she's chosen, and Gale becomes angry because of the injustice of the reaping process. Katniss explains that, at age twelve, your name is entered into the drawing once; at thirteen, it's entered twice; and so on up until age eighteen. But you can choose to have your name entered again in exchange for a tessera, a year's supply of grain and oil for one person. Poor people often need tesserae to survive, so the children of the poor end up having their names entered numerous times. Katniss, who is sixteen, will have her name in twenty times, and Gale, who is eighteen, will have his in forty-two times. Katniss's sister, Prim, is only twelve and has taken no tesserae, so her name is only in once. Katniss returns home, and after she gets ready, goes with her mother and Prim to the town square. That's where the reaping, which is televised and treated like a festive event, takes place in their district.

In the square, the mayor gives a speech that provides the history of the Hunger Games. Struck by droughts, storms, rising seas, and other natural problems, North America essentially dissolved, and the country of Panem rose up in its place. Panem was formed of a Capitol and thirteen districts, but the districts eventually rebelled. The Capitol defeated the districts, with the thirteenth being so badly destroyed that it ceased to exist. To punish the districts and remind them of their powerlessness, the Capitol holds the Hunger Games, in which a male and female "tribute" between twelve and eighteen from each district must fight to the death in a large outdoor arena. The tribute that survives wins, and that tribute's district receives extra food. Haymitch Abernathy, one of only two people from District 12 to have ever won the Hunger Games and the only one still living, comes out on stage. He is drunk and tries to hug Effie Trinket, a public figure who acts as an escort to District 12's tributes. Effie Trinket then draws the name of the first tribute: Primrose Everdeen.

SUMMARY: CHAPTER 2

As Prim walks up to the stage, Katniss, in a panic, rushes forward and shouts that she is volunteering as tribute. A volunteer is allowed to take the place of the person whose name is drawn, but this never happens in District 12. Katniss and Prim embrace, and Gale has to pull Prim away from Katniss. Katniss fights back any sign of emotion because crying will make the other tributes think she's weak. Effie Trinket asks for a round of applause, but the crowd remains silent and offers only a gesture of respect to Katniss. Haymitch falls off the stage while offering his congratulations.

The name of the boy tribute is drawn and it's Peeta Mellark. Katniss thinks about her interaction with Peeta years earlier. Her father had just died, and her mother fell into severe depression. They had run out of money and food—starvation is common in District 12, she says—and Katniss had wandered into the lane behind the shops of the wealthier townspeople. She searched the trash bins but found nothing. Suddenly, from the back door of the bakery, a woman was screaming at her to leave. Peeta, who was in Katniss's grade, was there, and he and the woman (his mother) went back inside. There was a commotion, then Peeta returned with two burned loaves of bread, his mother yelling behind him to feed them to the pigs. He had a welt on his cheek where his mother had hit him. He cautiously threw the loaves to Katniss instead. Katniss brought the bread home and fed her family. It made her hopeful they wouldn't starve, and she wondered if he had burned the bread on purpose to help her, despite knowing his mother would hit him for it. Later, she saw Peeta at the same time that she saw the first dandelion of spring. Recalling that dandelions are edible, she realized she would have to use the skills her father taught her to keep herself and her family alive, and she associates this realization with Peeta.

SUMMARY: CHAPTER 3

Katniss is escorted into the Justice Building and left in a room. Her mother and sister are brought in to say their good-byes, and Katniss makes her mother promise not to fall apart again. She tells them she loves them as they're led out. Peter Mellark's father, the baker, comes in. Katniss often trades him squirrels for bread. He gives Katniss cookies and promises to make sure Prim will be fed. Next, Madge, Katniss's friend from school, enters. She gives Katniss a pin with a gold bird in the center and asks Katniss to wear it into the arena. Last, Gale enters. He tells Katniss to find a bow if she can, and he says he won't let Katniss's family starve.

Katniss is driven to a train station where she meets Peeta, and they board a train and begin their journey to the Capitol. Katniss says District 12 is in what used to be Appalachia. It is still a coal mining area, as it was hundreds of years earlier. The Capitol is in what used to be the Rockies. Katniss realizes the pin Madge gave her is of a mockingjay, a type of bird that the Capitol once bred to spy on rebels in the districts. It could remember and repeat entire conversations, but when the rebels found out, they started using the birds to feed the Capitol false information. The Capitol stopped breeding the birds, but they survived. The pin is a small sign of rebellion. Katniss and Peeta have dinner with Effie Trinket on the train and they watch recaps of the reapings from the various districts. When Katniss and Peeta joke about Haymitch's drunkenness, Effie says they shouldn't be laughing because Haymitch is the one who is going to be advising them and getting them sponsors. Just then Haymitch comes in drunk, vomits, and falls in the mess.

ANALYSIS

In the first three chapters, we are introduced to some of the book's main characters, notably Katniss Everdeen, the protagonist of the novel. We also learn all the basic facts about the world in which the story takes place. Katniss is a sixteen-year-old girl living in what is essentially a dystopia, a fictional political state in which life is awful

(George Orwell's *1984* is also a dystopian novel). The book is set at some unspecified time in the future, when the countries of North America as we currently know them have dissolved. The cause of this dissolution isn't fully explained, but Katniss does talk about the natural disasters that led to it. Among them are rising sea levels and severe storms, which suggest global warming played a role, as those are two of the most serious consequences scientists predict warming will cause. We also know there are widespread food shortages. The government of Panem, the country that rose up after North America's collapse, is totalitarian. It monitors the speech and actions of its citizens and mercilessly punishes anything it construes as dissent. The Hunger Games that give the book its title are the ultimate expression of its mercilessness and its power over its citizens.

But life is also terrible for the people of District 12 for more immediate reasons. Few people, we learn, have enough to eat. Many are malnourished, and death by starvation is common. Moreover, the main industry in the region is coal mining, which is notoriously difficult and dangerous work. Katniss describes the miners, both men and women, heading to work with hunched shoulders and swollen knuckles, suggesting how physically hard the job is. We also know that both Katniss's and Gale's fathers died from an explosion in the mine. District 12 is in what's presently known as Appalachia, which is among the poorest regions in the modern United States, and from Katniss's description it seems the district is among the poorest regions of Panem.

The wealth of the government stands in direct contrast to the poverty of the people of District 12, and this inequality between rich and poor is a theme that continues throughout the novel. Most notably, the poorest of every district have an added hardship in that it is typically their children who become tributes in the Hunger Games, since they are the ones who take tesserae in exchange for entering their names more times in the Hunger Games drawing. The contrast between those who have money and those who don't becomes more prominent when Katniss has her first encounter with the government's wealth just after the reaping ceremony. She's taken to a room in the Justice Building that she says is the richest place she's ever been in, and she marvels at the luxury of it, particularly the plush velvet furniture. Katniss only knows what velvet is because her mother has a dress with a velvet collar, a detail that underscores how little her family has by comparison. Another such detail is mentioned on the tribute train: Katniss has her first shower, something she could never do at home because they have no hot water unless they boil it. Later, she gorges herself at dinner, having never had so much food in front of her before.

Katniss is very much a product of her dystopian environment, and her character is revealed gradually throughout these chapters, notably in her language. We learn that, though she is only a teenager, she is the primary caretaker in her family. More than anything, she is responsible for keeping them fed. She gets food from foraging and hunting, and as a result she has no qualms about killing animals. In fact, because of her constant exposure to death, she seems desensitized to it. This attitude is evident at the very start of the story, in her willingness to drown her sister's cat, Buttercup, when it first came to them. It also appears when she talks about the human suffering and deaths she's witnessed, in her own life as she sees people starving and in the televised Hunger Games. She is very unemotional describing these scenes, presenting the facts and not elaborating on her feelings about them. It is clear she finds them horrible, but not shocking. She treats them as part of her environment rather than as abnormalities.

We also learn about Katniss's family relationships. Her father was obviously a role model for her, and it's clear the pain of his death hasn't totally abated. She says she still wakes up at night frequently, dreaming of the explosion that killed him and screaming for him to run. Her relationship with her mother, meanwhile, is fraught with mixed feelings. She still clearly resents her mother for falling apart emotionally when Katniss's father was killed. Katniss was only eleven at the time, but she was forced to take on the responsibility of feeding the family. As a result, she had to use the hunting and foraging skills her father taught her to become the new provider for the family. Notably, this uncomfortable position has endowed her with valuable survival skills that will help her later during the Hunger Games, and Gale even points out that hunting a human shouldn't be too different from hunting game. Katniss's role as caretaker is most pronounced when she deals with Prim. Katniss has not allowed Prim to take out a tessera, thereby trying to keep her odds of being selected as tribute low. Despite these low odds, Katniss worries about her. She treats Prim with a gentleness we don't see her exhibit anywhere else, and she says explicitly she would do anything to protect Prim.

Katniss's memory of her encounter with Peeta is also significant as it creates a conflict within Katniss that she will have to deal with later. She essentially credits Peeta's giving her the two loaves of bread years earlier with restoring her hope and saving her after her father's death. Without this act, she thinks she and her family might have starved, and she also thinks about how Peeta was present when she realized she would have to take care of her family. Now she connects her survival during that difficult period with Peeta and his uncommon act of kindness. The irony of the situation is that she may eventually have to kill this boy who helped keep her alive, since only one person can survive the Hunger Games. Her only hope, she thinks, is that someone else will kill him first, suggesting she feels she may not be able to do so if the situation arises.

These first chapters establish the theme of suffering as entertainment, one of the main themes of the novel. The Hunger Games, we learn, are a televised contest in which children fight one another to the death, and they are watched by all of Panem. Their main attraction is the actual, real-life suffering experienced by the tributes. In this way, the Hunger Games recall the gladiatorial games of ancient Rome, but they function as essentially an exaggerated, dystopian version of reality television. They are dissimilar from reality television, however, in that the government mandates them, and it's clear that many of the residents of District 12, and likely those of the other poor districts, view them as a form of oppression. Indeed, the government intends them as a reminder of the districts' defeat and powerlessness. The forced sense of festivity that accompanies the Games, evident in the public ceremony of the reaping in these chapters, only makes them more grotesque and underscores how insensitive the Capitol is to the lives of Panem's ordinary citizens. In the Capitol and the wealthier districts, on the other hand, the Games are immensely popular and the greatest form of entertainment the citizens have.

Another main theme, the importance of appearances, also begins taking shape in this section. Katniss repeatedly forces herself not to cry, knowing that everything she does is being televised, and the other tributes will take tears as a sign of weakness. She feels she must present herself in a certain way so as not to make herself a target of the other tributes, who may look at her as an easy kill. By controlling how others perceive her, Katniss essentially hopes to gain a strategic advantage, or at least not be at a disadvantage. To this end, she frequently masks her true feelings, instead showing the cameras only what she wants them to see, and she must manage both what she experiences internally and how she wants to look to the outside world. The theme suggests that appearances, particularly as they are presented in the media, can be as important as reality.

CHAPTERS 4–6

SUMMARY: CHAPTER 4

Peeta volunteers to clean up Haymitch, who is drunk and has fallen in his own vomit. While Katniss sits in her room, she wonders why Peeta did this, then realizes he may just be kind. She decides this is more dangerous to her than an unlikable Peeta and determines not to get any closer with him. When she throws the cookies his father gave her out the window, they land in a field of dandelions, and she remembers gathering dandelions with Prim after she realized she would have to feed her family. Her mother, who is an apothecary, had a book describing plants that could be used for healing, and in it she found notes, made by her father, about which plants were edible. The next day, she went into the woods alone for the first time and began hunting and foraging regularly to keep her family alive. What she caught or collected that she didn't need, she would trade or sell at the Hob. One day, she noticed some katniss, the plant she was named after, in a pond. She dug up the edible roots, and that night she and her family ate until they were full. Her mother began to return to normal as well. Katniss, however, never fully forgave her mother her weakness, and their relationship was never the same. Katniss wonders what her mother and Prim are doing at home and falls asleep.

In the morning she goes to the train's dining car. Effie, Peeta, and Haymitch are there. Haymitch is already drinking, and Peeta gets angry with him because he's supposed to be advising them. He slaps the drink out of Haymitch's hand. Haymitch punches him, and Katniss stabs her knife into the table between his hand and the liquor bottle. Haymitch wonders if he's got fighters this year and asks Katniss what else she can do with a knife. She pulls it out of the table and throws skillfully into the wall. If they don't interfere with his drinking, Haymitch says he'll help them. His first piece of advice is that whatever the stylists do to them, they shouldn't resist. The train finally arrives at the Capitol. Katniss and Peeta are amazed at the grandeur and strangeness of it. The people all have bizarre hair and painted faces. Peeta waves to the people gathered to see the tributes coming in. He says he's waving because some of them may be rich, and Katniss realizes he may be planning a way to survive the Games, making him a threat to her.

SUMMARY: CHAPTER 5

In the Capitol, a team of people wax Katniss's body hair to prepare her for her stylist, Cinna. Cinna is quiet and modest. It's his first year working as a stylist for the Hunger Games, and to Katniss's surprise, he requested the tributes of the impoverished District 12. It is typical for the tributes to dress in a style that reflects their district, and Cinna says since District 12's industry is coal mining, Katniss and Peeta's costumes will reflect coal's main function, which is to burn. Her costume will be lit with a synthetic flame, and Cinna calls her "the girl who was on fire." In their matching costumes—an unusual touch as tributes are rarely made to match—Katniss and Peeta are escorted to a main plaza in the city, where they will go before the huge audience. The other districts' tributes all have their turns, then just before Katniss and Peeta emerge, Cinna lights them and tells them to hold hands. They emerge and are instantly a sensation. The crowd loves them, and because of Cinna's work, they are the most memorable tributes of the night.

SUMMARY: CHAPTER 6

At the Training Center, where the tributes stay until the Games begin, Effie Trinket talks enthusiastically about Katniss and Peeta. Katniss, meanwhile, is in awe of how luxurious her room is. It's larger than her house and has all sorts of automated features, notably in the shower and closet. Katniss finds everyone, including the stylists, in the dining room for dinner. The servers are all young people dressed in white tunics. Katniss, who has had some wine, says she knows one of them, a girl with red hair, then realizes this person is associated with a bad memory. Effie snaps at her, saying she can't possibly know an Avox. Haymitch explains that an Avox is someone who committed a crime and had their tongue cut out. Katniss says it must be a mistake, and Peeta covers for her by saying the Avox girl resembles someone from their school. Everyone talks about their success at the ceremony, then Haymitch tells Katniss and Peeta to go get some sleep. Their training begins the next day.

Katniss and Peeta go to the roof, where they can speak without being overheard. There's an electrified field around it so tributes can't jump off, and Peeta leads Katniss to a garden where wind chimes and the wind will cover their voices. Katniss says she and Gale were hunting in the woods one day when they saw a ragged-looking girl and boy running in terror. A hovercraft appeared and captured the girl in a net. It hauled her up instantly, then shot the boy through with a spear that had a cable attached and hauled his body up too. Then it disappeared. Katniss says for a moment, before the girl was taken, she locked eyes with her, but Katniss did nothing. The memory haunts her. They go back inside because it's cold, and Peeta asks Katniss if Gale is a relative. He also asks if Gale came to say good-bye when she left. She says he did, but so did Peeta's father. Peeta mentions that his father knew Katniss's mother. They say good night, and in her room Katniss sees the redheaded Avox. She asks the girl to take some clothes to Cinna, and as she falls asleep, wonders if the girl will enjoy watching her die in the Games.

ANALYSIS

The clash between Katniss's poor upbringing and the wealth of the Capitol continues throughout these chapters. In Chapter 4, we see how Katniss learned to forage, and she describes how, after the meal of katniss roots she gathered, she and her family felt full for the first time in months. A few paragraphs later, the story returns to the present, and Katniss sits down to a large breakfast of eggs, ham, fried potatoes, bread, and other things. The theme continues in Chapter 5, when Katniss meets with Cinna. At the press of a button, Cinna summons a giant meal, prompting Katniss to consider the many days of effort it would take to prepare the same meal herself at home. The scene highlights exactly how much the people of the Capitol have compared to those in the districts, particularly the poorer districts like District 12.

The theme of the importance of appearances has a significant role in this section. Chapter 5 is devoted entirely to Katniss's preparation for the tributes' introduction ceremony and the look Cinna creates for her. The costumes the stylists create make Katniss (and Peeta) exceptional, rather than just two more tributes taking part in the Games. In the context of the story, it's important for Katniss and Peeta to stand out because that helps them to attract sponsors, who can give them useful gifts during the Games that may ultimately mean the difference between survival and death. But it also demonstrates that appearance can be more important than reality in any media spectacle. The stylists' costumes turn Katniss and Peeta into media sensations, and the people watching the Hunger Games prefer this manufactured spectacle to the reality of the situation, that Katniss, Peeta, and the other tributes are mostly just frightened children. The costumes and ceremony essentially hide reality in entertainment.

In addition, the way Haymitch and the stylists tell Katniss and Peeta to present themselves in this section becomes part of a strategy to control what the other tributes think of the pair, again emphasizing how important appearances can be. Their matching costumes and their holding hands make them appear to be a couple, an unusual approach given that only one person can win the Games and they will essentially be enemies once inside the arena. By contrast, the other tributes are presented as individuals, even if they are from the same district and appear together during the opening ceremony. It is unclear at this point what the ultimate purpose of this strategy is, but the intent is clearly to give Katniss and Peeta an advantage in the Games.

The Avoxes in Chapter 6 further highlight the brutality and totalitarian nature of Panem's government. The Avoxes are considered criminals, and when Haymitch explains that the redheaded Avox that Katniss recognizes is probably a traitor of some sort, it suggests that their crimes are against the state (rather than against another citizen, as in a theft). Panem punishes them brutally by cutting out their tongues, literally and symbolically silencing them, and essentially making them slaves. They are isolated from those around them as well and only spoken to when being given an order. It's unclear what crime this Avox committed, but simply that she is a young girl suggests the punishment was excessive. The boy Katniss saw the Avox running away with was punished just as savagely, shot through with a spear.

The section also elaborates on Katniss's backstory and provides more insight into her character. Katniss began venturing under the fence to hunt and forage in the woods, then to trade in the Hob, when she was still very young. From her retelling of that period, she was clearly very afraid, yet she forced herself to do what was necessary to survive and keep her family fed, suggesting tremendous inner strength and resolve. Moreover, she's intelligent, as she was able to learn everything she needed to find food with the help of the book she found with her father's notes. The story makes it clear that Katniss is a character with impressive resourcefulness, and though it's uncertain at this point how these traits will help her in the Hunger Games, they are undoubtedly assets she will rely on.

Katniss's inner conflict regarding Peeta continues to mount in this section. Peeta's kindness toward Haymitch initially makes her wonder if he has some ulterior motive, but when she realizes he may just be kind she finds this idea even more difficult to tolerate. She knows she may have to kill Peeta at some point, and thinking of him as a kind person only makes that thought more repulsive. She determines to have no more contact with him, even throwing away the cookies his father gave her, in an effort to distance herself from him as much as possible, but by the end of the section she has only drawn closer to him. He helps her out of her situation with the Avox by lying and saying the Avox looks like someone in their school, thus ingratiating himself with her even more. At the end of the night, rather than pull away, she ends up confiding in him about the Avox girl, and he lets her use his jacket when she gets cold, a gesture that suggests he cares about her. Katniss accepting his jacket carries its own message: she has let her guard down and let Peeta in.

CHAPTERS 7–9

SUMMARY: CHAPTER 7

It is the first day of training. For three days, the twenty-four tributes all practice together, then on the final afternoon they perform in private in front of the Gamemakers, the officials who run the Games. Haymitch asks Katniss and Peeta if they want to train together or separately, in case one has a secret skill she or he might not want the other to know about. Peeta already knows Katniss is an excellent hunter, and Katniss feels surprised at the thought that Peeta sometimes thinks about her. Ultimately they decide to train together. Haymitch wants to know about their strengths. Katniss's is obviously with a bow, and Peeta is strong and an excellent wrestler. But Peeta feels he has no chance. He says Katniss has no idea the effect she can have, and his mother even praised Katniss over him, calling her a survivor. Katniss says she couldn't have survived without Peeta, and from Peeta's reaction she realizes he remembers giving her the bread those years ago. Haymitch tells them not to reveal their strengths until the private session with the Gamemakers and to be sure they're always seen together.

At training, Katniss watches the other tributes. Almost all are bigger than she is, though many are clearly underfed. The tributes from the wealthier districts are all healthy. Some of them, called Career Tributes, train all their lives to compete in the Games. The training area has different stations with instructors, and the Career Tributes go right to the stations with the deadliest weapons. Katniss and Peeta go to a station where they learn various knots. Next they move to the camouflage station, and Peeta picks it up quickly because he decorates the cakes in his father's bakery. Over the next three days, they visit more stations while the Gamemakers—twenty or so men and women—watch from the stands and take notes. Peeta and Katniss stay together the whole time, making small talk. At lunch one day Peeta explains that each district has its own distinct bread and shows them all to Katniss. In training they also notice one of the female tributes, a small young girl from District 11 named Rue, watching them.

Katniss is last to have her private session with the Gamemakers. She selects a bow from the weapons available, but it's different from her bow at home and takes some practice before she can use it accurately. She takes a few difficult shots to impress the Gamemakers, but notices that most of them are focused on a roasted pig that's just arrived at their table. She becomes furious, knowing her life is at stake in the Games, and fires an arrow straight toward the Gamemakers that skewers the apple in the pig's mouth. Then she walks out.

SUMMARY: CHAPTER 8

As soon as she leaves she begins to panic, wondering if they will punish her for her defiance. The Gamemakers score the tributes from one to twelve based on their performance, and Katniss is certain her score will be very low. That could make it difficult to get sponsors, and their gifts are critical for survival in the arena. She locks herself in her room and doesn't come out until Effie calls her to dinner. At the table, everyone wants to know how Peeta and Katniss did. Katniss tells her story, and everyone is shocked but Haymitch, who finds it amusing. When the scores are announced, Peeta gets an eight and Katniss gets an eleven. She's stunned, but Haymitch says they probably liked her temper.

In the morning, Katniss lies in bed for a time after waking and thinks of when she first met Gale. She was in the woods hunting and saw several rabbits hanging from snares. When she went to inspect them, Gale came forward. She'd seen him before: his father died in the same mine blast as hers and they both attended the memorial. They talked about hunting at first, and over time they became a team. Katniss thinks of how close they are and misses him. She has with Gale what she pretends to have with Peeta. Effie calls her down for breakfast, and when she arrives at the table, Haymitch says there's been a change in strategy: Peeta has asked to be coached separately.

Summary: Chapter 9

Katniss feels betrayed by Peeta but also relieved they don't have to keep up the appearance of being good friends. In preparation for a televised interview she and the other tributes will be doing the next day, Katniss goes with Effie for instruction on "presentation." Effie makes Katniss wear high heels, corrects her posture, and tells her to make sure she's always smiling. It's important that the audience like Katniss. Next, Katniss meets with Haymitch. He says the impression she makes may determine what sponsors he can get her, but she comes across as hostile. Haymitch tries to get her to seem friendly but eventually gives up. Katniss has dinner in her room that night and smashes dishes in a rage. The redheaded Avox comes in and wipes Katniss's face and hands, which she cut on a broken dish. Katniss says she should have tried to save her, but the Avox gestures that Katniss would only have ended up like her. Katniss helps her clean up, then goes to sleep.

The next morning, Katniss meets with Cinna. He puts her in a dress covered in jewels that, in the light, give the impression of little flames. He asks if Katniss is ready for her interview, but she says she's awful. He tells her to be herself, since everyone already loves her spirit, and generally comforts her. The time for the interviews comes. Each tribute gets three minutes. Katniss's turn arrives and she goes up on the stage. The host is Caesar Flickerman, who does the interviews every year. Katniss does very well, coming off as very charming and even feminine. The crowd loves her. When she's done, she watches Peeta go on next. Caesar asks if he has a girlfriend, and Peeta says no, but that there is a girl he's had a crush on as long as he can remember. Caesar says she can't turn him down if he wins, but Peeta says winning won't help him. The girl he's thinking of came to the Games with him.

Analysis

Katniss's training continues in this section, and again emphasizes the importance of appearances. Katniss's instruction this time is not on weapons or survival techniques, but on how she should present herself. If she is to have a good chance at surviving the Games, she must win over the public and the sponsors, who can give her gifts that may prove critical during the Hunger Games. Internally, she despises the Hunger Games and everyone who views them as entertainment, but she knows it's best to follow Haymitch's instruction and keep those feelings hidden. Moreover, she needs to be likable in every regard: not just in what she says, but also in how she looks and comports herself. Effie even instructs her on such niceties as posture, hand gestures, sitting properly, and how to smile. Haymitch also makes sure Katniss and Peeta are always seen as a pair rather than as individuals, and at the end of the section, when Peeta reveals that he has had a crush on Katniss for years, Haymitch's reasons for keeping them together all the time start to become more clear.

The spectacle surrounding the Hunger Games, notably the interviews Katniss, Peeta, and the other tributes must give, again treat suffering as a form of entertainment. The tributes are treated as if their selection for the Hunger Games were an honor. But the unspoken reason for their popularity is people know that all but one of them will be dead within a matter of days or weeks. The implied reason for even having interviews with the tributes is that the death of an anonymous competitor is not as compelling as the death of a person whom the audience has gotten to know. The Games are actually more entertaining this way. Because these interviews are only entertaining if the tributes appear happy (a tribute distraught over his probable death would likely not be fun for an audience to watch), the tributes are expected to be cheerful and polite. Unhappy tributes also don't win sponsors, so as a result, the tributes must suppress whatever negative emotions they're feeling for the sake of keeping up the entertainment of the Games.

We also see more examples of the inequality between rich and poor in this section. The Career Tributes, those tributes from wealthy districts who have been trained for years to take part in the Hunger Games, have several advantages over the tributes from poorer districts. First, they are well-fed, making them noticeably healthier and stronger than most of the other tributes. Second, they are trained to use the weapons the tributes may find in the arena. During the public training session, Katniss even points out how clumsy the normal tributes seem with many of the weapons contrasted with the Career Tributes, who handle the weapons easily and competently. The result of this inequality between the wealthier districts and the poor districts is that the tributes of the wealthier districts seem far more likely to survive, and even for those that don't, their lives were likely to have been less difficult leading up to the Hunger Games.

Ironically, however, the hardships Katniss has had to navigate growing up give her her own distinct set of skills, which may, in the end, put her at an advantage. For the past five years, Katniss has had to hunt and forage to feed herself and her family. It is not certain how the skills she's acquired as a result may help her during the Games, but the presence of the station on edible plants during the public training suggests the tributes will likely have to know how to find food in the wilderness. Katniss, then, will have a better chance at survival than a tribute whose family was wealthy enough to simply buy food. Katniss also notes that, while many of the other tributes from the poorer districts are bigger than she is, they also look a bit sickly, whereas she is in very good shape from the daily work of hunting. Perhaps most importantly, Katniss's hunting experience makes her an expert with a bow. While she might not be able to physically overpower the other tributes, she can certainly defend herself or kill from a distance.

This section provides more insight into Peeta's character as well. For instance, we learn what strengths he possesses that might be of use to him during the Games: He is physically strong, he's an excellent wrestler who excels at hand-to-hand combat, and he's also adept at camouflage. In addition, we find out that he's been paying attention to Katniss for a long time. He remembers the incident when he gave her the loaves of bread, and he's aware of her hunting skills because he's often eaten the squirrels she's sold his father. When he tells Haymitch that Katniss has no idea of the effect she can have, we also get a hint that he may have a romantic interest in her. This suspicion is confirmed at the end of the section, when Peeta tells Caesar Flickerman that the girl he's had a crush on for years is the same one who came to the Hunger Games with him. (Notably, it's not clear why he asks to be trained separately, as this desire seems to contradict his feelings for Katniss.)

While we learn how Peeta feels about Katniss, we also learn more about Katniss's relationship with Gale. She describes their first meeting, and she hints that she found him immediately appealing, saying when he smiled it transformed him into someone you want to know. They developed first into hunting partners, then into friends, and while they never had a romantic relationship of any sort, it's clear that Katniss feels strongly about him. At one point, while lying in bed, she misses him and thinks of how comfortable she feels with him. Significantly, she compares her relationship with Gale to her relationship with Peeta, and recognizes that she genuinely has with Gale what she and Peeta pretend to have in front of the other tributes and the cameras. Peeta's revelation that he has a romantic interest in Katniss establishes the beginnings of a new problem for her. She misses Gale and feels that's he truly her friend, but he's not around. At the same time, she must pretend to be very close with Peeta, but she doesn't want to be close to him because they will be enemies once inside the arena. Peeta, meanwhile, has genuine feelings for her. So while she craves the friendship and closeness Gale can offer, she can't have it, but the comfort she can have from Peeta she doesn't want.

CHAPTERS 10–12

SUMMARY: CHAPTER 10

The crowd goes crazy over Peeta's declaration of love for Katniss. When the interviews are over, Katniss encounters Peeta and shoves him, making him fall over an urn and cut his hands on the broken shards. Katniss says he had no right to share his feelings about her. Effie, Haymitch, and some others arrive. Haymitch says Katniss shouldn't be angry, because Peeta made her look desirable, something she couldn't achieve on her own. They add that they didn't tell her because they wanted her reaction to be real. Katniss realizes Haymitch is right, she may gain an advantage with sponsors now, and she apologizes to Peeta.

Katniss and Peeta say their good-byes to Haymitch and Effie. In the morning they will leave for the arena. Haymitch tells them that when the gong sounds and the Games officially begin, they should run away. They aren't prepared for the bloodbath at the Cornucopia. That night, Katniss has difficulty sleeping. She finds Peeta on the roof. He says he wants to die as himself, not as some kind of monster, and wishes he could think of a way to show the Capitol they don't own him. In the morning, Katniss boards a hovercraft. She is injected with a tracker, and with Cinna, departs for the arena. When they arrive, she and Cinna go into an underground room. She dresses in the outfit given to all the tributes, then Cinna takes out the gold mockingjay pin and puts it on her. He reminds her of Haymitch's advice: run, then find water. He says if he could bet, his money would be on her, and he wishes good luck to the girl who was on fire. Then Katniss is raised up through a cylinder into the arena, and the seventy-fourth Hunger Games officially begin.

SUMMARY: CHAPTER 11

The tributes must wait sixty seconds before they are released. While she waits, Katniss surveys the field. Just in front of her is a small tarp. In the Cornucopia, a large structure literally shaped like a cornucopia, she sees a tent pack and a bow and arrows. She thinks she might be able to reach the bow before anyone else but remembers Haymitch's instructions to get away and find water. She's preparing to run when she notices Peeta. He is looking at her and shaking his head as if telling her "no." The gong sounds, and because Katniss was distracted by Peeta, she misses her chance. She grabs the tarp and decides to sprint to an orange backpack farther in. She gets there at the same time as another boy, and while they struggle for it, blood sprays Katniss's face. The boy falls, and Katniss sees a knife in his back. She runs for the woods while putting the backpack on, and a knife hits the pack and lodges firmly in it. Briefly she looks back to see the tributes fighting. Several already lie dead on the ground. She continues into the woods and doesn't stop for a long time while she looks for water.

During the Games, a cannon sounds to mark the death of a tribute, and once the main battle is over, Katniss hears eleven cannon shots. That means thirteen tributes remain. At night they'll play the Capitol's anthem and project the images of the dead into the sky for everyone to see. She wonders if Peeta is alive, then checks the contents of the backpack. It contains a sleeping bag, a little food, a bottle of iodine for purifying water, an empty bottle, and some other items. Katniss was hoping for water, and she knows she won't last long without it. There was a lake by the Cornucopia, and she's worried it may be the only water source in the arena since it's sure to be guarded by Career Tributes. Eventually it gets dark, so Katniss makes her bed in a tree and uses her belt to secure herself to a branch. The faces of the dead tributes are projected one after another in the sky, and Katniss is relieved that Peeta is not among them.

Someone starts a fire nearby. Katniss lies in her sleeping bag, and when it's almost dawn, she hears several people running toward the fire. A girl pleads and then screams, and Katniss realizes several tributes are hunting in a pack. They stop a few yards from her tree and discuss why the cannon hasn't sounded to announce the girl's death. The voices belong to some of the Career Tributes, but another voice says he'll go back to make sure she's dead. It belongs to Peeta.

SUMMARY: CHAPTER 12

Katniss is shocked that Peeta joined the Careers. She sees he is badly bruised and realizes he must have fought at the Cornucopia. While Peeta goes to check on the girl, the Career Tributes talk about killing. They wonder why Katniss scored an eleven in training, and as

Peeta returns Katniss realizes he hasn't told them about her skill with a bow. The cannon sounds and the Careers move off. Katniss climbs down and is on the move again. Checking the snares she set the day before, she finds a rabbit, which she cooks, then eats as she walks opposite the direction the Careers went. As she travels, she becomes increasingly exhausted and dehydrated. Waking the next morning, she has an awful headache and her joints hurt. Though severely fatigued, she continues searching for water. At one point she begins to curse Haymitch. She knows she must have a sponsor and Haymitch could easily send her water, but then she realizes he may not be doing so for a reason. Eventually she collapses and thinks she can't go on, until she realizes she is lying in mud. Crawling through a tangle of plants, she finds a small pond. She rests there for several hours and rehydrates, then finds a tree to sleep in. In the middle of the night, she's awakened by a huge fire moving toward her.

ANALYSIS

Katniss's relationship with Peeta changes substantially over the course of this section. Katniss has just learned that Peeta has romantic feelings for her, and initially she feels she is being used. She becomes angry with Peeta as a result, going so far as to shove him over an urn of flowers. Although Peeta doesn't explicitly say so, he clearly feels hurt by this response because it shows that Katniss doesn't reciprocate his feelings. Katniss eventually calms down and apologizes, but Peeta remains cold toward her, and whatever intimacy they had established is now gone. Katniss later begins to seriously distrust Peeta when she realizes that he's teamed with the Career Tributes; that he stayed and fought at the Cornucopia, suggesting he had planned to do so all along; and that he may be helping the Careers to find her. But Katniss also considers that Peeta shook his head at her at the Cornucopia, which may have been him watching out for her welfare, and that he didn't tell the Careers about her skill with a bow, preserving her advantage should she find one. The result is that Katniss feels ambivalent and isn't sure where she stands with Peeta.

Peeta's actions in these chapters offer new insight into his character. Whereas previously Peeta seemed to be kind and even gentle, we now see he is capable of being savage if need be. When Katniss overhears the Careers talking, they note that Peeta is handy with a knife, and knowing that Peeta fought at the Cornucopia, it suggests

Peeta may have killed one or more of the other tributes. Moreover, he finishes off the girl that his group attacked after they realize she hasn't died. Peeta, however, seems to behave this way out of necessity only. Before he and Katniss entered the arena, he acknowledged that he would kill if he had to, but he also wanted to remain himself and not become a monster. He also still appears to feel a sense of loyalty to Katniss, which is evident in him not telling the Career Tributes about her ability with a bow. He seems to be doing what he feels is necessary to stay alive but does not want to betray Katniss, even if doing so would benefit him by eliminating her as a competitor.

Peeta's comment the night before leaving the Training Center, that he will kill just like everybody else but also wants to show the Capitol they don't own him, brings up a paradox that affects most of the tributes and in fact many of the people in Panem's districts. Most of the tributes are not Career Tributes, and if Katniss and Peeta are any indication, they are predominantly ordinary teenagers who are horrified at the idea of having to kill another person. The Capitol, however, has put them in a position where they must kill or be killed themselves. Peeta says he wants to preserve his identity, but he acknowledges that he will essentially be doing what the Capitol wants him to. He wonders how he can preserve his identity in such a position, when he is no longer in full control of his fate, and at this point he has no clear answer. Though to a less severe degree, the people in Panem's districts face a similar problem in that they live under a totalitarian government that doesn't allow them to express their opinions or behave as they like. These people's identities, similarly, are not entirely under their control.

The Hunger Games officially begin in this section with a quick flurry of brutality, but Katniss is notably not distraught at the deaths of the other tributes. Just after the Games begin, for instance, Katniss sees a boy die right in front of her and is splattered across the face with his blood, yet only a few moments later she grins and jokes to herself after a knife lodges in her backpack. This reaction demonstrates a sense of ease rather than terror or horror. Neither does the sight of several dead tributes at the Cornucopia seem to startle her, nor the death of the girl who starts the fire near her on the first night. As earlier chapters have hinted, Katniss appears to be generally desensitized to death. No reason is ever stated explicitly, but her upbringing offers clues. Katniss has been hunting for years, which not only entails killing animals, but cleaning and sometimes butchering them as well, meaning blood and open wounds wouldn't be new to her. When she hunts, of course, it is for animals, but Katniss has also seen a great deal of human suffering. She's noted that it is common for people to starve to death in District 12, and she has seen numerous people injured or maimed in mine accidents brought in to her mother for emergency care. As a result, these sights are not totally alien to her, and she regards them with little interest.

The skills and abilities Katniss learned from her sometimes impoverished upbringing come in handy right away in the Games. Because of her experience hunting and foraging, Katniss is able to set a trap with the wire she finds in her backpack, catching a rabbit that provides invaluable nutrition as she searches for water. She is also accustomed to walking long distances and going with little food, and she knows the woods. When she starts to feel hungry, she cuts some of the rough outer bark off a pine tree and scrapes up a bunch of the soft inner bark, allowing her to hold off hunger a little longer. These factors play directly into her ability to endure until she finds a source of water other than the lake, and they essentially keep her alive. While it is obvious that the other tributes pose a threat, it becomes clear that the greater, or at least more immediate, threat may simply be surviving in a foreign environment without any food or water readily available.

CHAPTERS 13–15

SUMMARY: CHAPTER 13

Katniss runs from the fire. It is so large that she knows it was the Gamemakers, not the tributes, who started it. They probably thought the audience was getting bored. She is choking on the smoke and begins to vomit uncontrollably, and just as she's recovering, a fireball explodes nearby. She runs, dodging the fireballs, but comes to a stop when she begins retching again. A fireball brushes her calf, scalding her. She manages to put the fire out, but her hands and calf are seriously injured. Eventually the attack ends and Katniss walks until she finds a small pool. The water soothes the burns. She knows she should keep going, but the pain is too great when she takes her leg out of the pool, so she spends the day there recovering. In the afternoon, however, she hears footsteps, and without any alternative she finds a tree and climbs as quickly as possible.

It's the five Careers and Peeta. Katniss calls down to them, knowing they're too heavy to climb to where she is. Katniss notices that a girl named Glimmer has the bow and arrows from the Cornucopia.

A large and dangerous looking boy named Cato begins climbing up after Katniss, but he falls out of the tree. Glimmer goes up next, but she doesn't get far before she must stop. She fires an arrow at Katniss, but she's incompetent with the bow and her shot misses. The group decides to wait Katniss out. Unable to go anywhere, Katniss prepares her bed in the tree. As night falls, she recognizes Rue, the girl tribute from District 11, in a nearby tree, and she realizes Rue has been there the whole time. Rue points at something above Katniss's head.

SUMMARY: CHAPTER 14

Katniss looks up and sees that Rue is pointing to a wasp's nest higher up. Katniss thinks it is probably a tracker jacker nest. Tracker jackers are another mutation created by the Capitol during the war with the districts. They will follow anything that disturbs them and try to kill it. Katniss thinks her only chance of escaping may be to drop the nest onto the tributes below. To avoid drawing the wasps to herself, she decides to saw the branch off during the anthem, which always plays before the dead tributes of the day are projected in the sky. When the anthem starts, Katniss climbs up and saws at the branch holding the nest, but the anthem ends before she finishes so she decides to wait until morning. When she gets back to her sleeping bag, she sees a gift that Haymitch must have gotten from her sponsors and sent during the anthem. It's a burn ointment, and it instantly soothes Katniss's hands and leg. Grateful, she falls asleep.

When she wakes, her burns have improved dramatically. She alerts Rue that she's going to drop the nest, and she hears Rue moving away by jumping from tree to tree. Katniss is stung a few times as she finishes cutting the branch, but the nest crashes to the ground and the group of tributes is immediately swarmed. Most of them run to the lake, but Glimmer is stung too many times and dies there, while another girl staggers off weakly, unlikely to make it very far. Katniss climbs down and runs back to the pool. The areas where she was stung have swelled and she submerges them in the water. Suddenly she remembers the bow Glimmer had, and she runs back to get it. She has to struggle to get the quiver of arrows free, and she hears someone crashing through the trees. Just as she raises the bow to defend herself she sees that it's Peeta. She thinks he's going to kill her, but he yells at her to run and shoves her. As she goes, she sees Cato arriving. Charging through the trees, Katniss begins to hallucinate badly from the venom, until finally she collapses in a hole and blacks out.

SUMMARY: CHAPTER 15

Katniss eventually awakens and realizes that a day or two have passed. Then she remembers that Peeta saved her life and wonders why he did it. She also remembers that she got the bow and arrows, and finally she feels like she has a chance in the Games. She goes in search of water, and within an hour, locates a stream. She is able to clean up and rest a little and hunt. As she sets her kill to cook, she hears a twig snap. It's Rue. Katniss asks if she wants to be her ally and invites her to eat. In return, Rue removes the venom from Katniss's stings with a remedy she knows involving the leaves of a plant. Rue tells Katniss about District 11. It's the agricultural district, but the workers aren't allowed to keep what they harvest. They're whipped if they're caught.

Katniss and Rue lay out all their equipment to take inventory, and Rue tells Katniss that what Katniss thought were sunglasses are really night-vision glasses. She tells Katniss how a mentally disabled boy in her district was killed for taking a pair. They climb a tree to sleep, and since Rue has nothing to keep her warm, they share a sleeping bag. Katniss tells her about Peeta saving her, and Rue points out that he's no longer with the Careers. She's been spying on their camp by the lake. The Careers have everything they need at their camp, so even though Katniss and Rue can feed themselves in the forest, it doesn't give them an advantage. Katniss says if the Careers' supplies were gone they wouldn't last long, and she starts devising a plan.

ANALYSIS

The fire attack on Katniss and the other tributes again brings up the theme of suffering as entertainment. Katniss suspects the Gamemakers started the fire because no tributes had died in some time and the audience at home would be getting bored. The Gamemakers, she believes, wanted to push the tributes together so they would be forced to fight. In that case, the Gamemakers intend to please their audience by causing the tributes greater distress, even though many of the tributes were already wounded and suffering by that point anyway. Katniss also believes that the fireball attack stopped before it killed her deliberately, because killing her would limit her entertainment value. She would no longer be a competitor and the audience at home wouldn't be able to see her struggling to survive, and ideally, battling the other tributes. In essence, the Gamemakers choose to prolong her suffering as a way of prolonging the entertainment of the audience. In each case, the tributes are treated essentially as commodities, rather than people; their purpose is to entertain.

Katniss is always aware that an audience and the Gamemakers are watching her, and she comments repeatedly in this section on what she imagines they're thinking. After the fire attack, she imagines what the Gamemakers' motivation was for halting the assault, and she realizes that there must have been another tribute near. Her logic proceeds from having watched the Hunger Games over the years and recognizing that the fireballs weren't necessarily intended to kill her but to push her into the vicinity of another tribute in order to create a fight. She also thinks the Gamemakers deliberately chose fire for the attack as a reference to her, "the girl who was on fire." Notably, Katniss even plays to the audience at home. When the Careers and Peeta arrive at the base of the tree she has climbed, she calls down to them as she thinks to herself that the audience at home will love it. Behind this awareness is the knowledge that, again, the Games are foremost entertainment for those watching at home. Though she certainly doesn't like it, Katniss understands this about the Games and it is never far from her mind.

We additionally learn about what life is like in another of the districts, District 11, and we see more examples of Panem's brutal treatment of its citizens. After they've allied with one another, Katniss learns from Rue about life in Panem's agricultural district, District 11. To Katniss's surprise, life in District 11 is as hard, if not harder, than life in District 12, where Katniss is from. Perhaps the greatest surprise to Katniss is that although much of Panem's food is being grown in District 11, many of its inhabitants still don't have enough to eat. As Rue explains, the government doesn't allow the people to keep any of the food they harvest, and to ensure that people don't steal, the government publicly whips anyone caught taking food. The government is so brutal, in fact, that Rue says it killed a mentally disabled boy who took a pair of night-vision glasses, the type Katniss found in her backpack. Katniss had assumed that, because her district was the poorest, life would be better in the other districts. What she learns is that the government of Panem makes life difficult everywhere.

Katniss's recovery of the bow, and her new alliance with Rue, mark a turning point for her in the Games. For the first time since the Games began, she feels somewhat secure. Having the bow makes her confident, and she thinks to herself that she is no longer prey for the other tributes. She even welcomes the thought of Cato attacking her as she knows she could easily take him down. Moreover, having Rue to talk to clearly brings her a sense of emotional comfort. Rue, as Katniss has noted since she first saw her, reminds Katniss very much of Prim, her little sister. She reminds Katniss of home, and she also provides the companionship Katniss has been missing without Peeta or Gale. With her burns healing and the knowledge that she and Rue can feed themselves without help from anyone else, Katniss comes to recognize the advantage she and Rue have over the other tributes. The only reason their experience hunting and foraging hasn't given them a distinct upper hand over the Careers is because the Careers took all the supplies they would need at the Cornucopia. At the end of the section, Katniss comes up with a plan to put their advantage into effect somehow (not yet revealed how) and decides to go on the offensive, a move that illustrates her newfound confidence.

Katniss's understanding of Peeta takes a new turn in this section and becomes more complicated when Peeta saves her life. Katniss had lost her trust in Peeta when she realized he had allied with the Careers. She had assumed he was helping them to find her in exchange for remaining alive longer himself. But when Peeta found Katniss weakened and disoriented by the wasp venom, he saved her rather than choosing to kill her or lead the Careers to her. Peeta clearly still feels a sense of loyalty to Katniss and he likely has genuine romantic feelings for her. Katniss, however, doesn't trust him, and as a result, she has difficulty understanding why he chose to help her. Up to this point, she has struggled at times to know when Peeta was being honest with her, about his romantic feelings for instance, and when he was playing to the audience as part of a strategy to get more sponsors. When Rue tells Katniss that Peeta's feelings weren't an act, Katniss assures her that they were an act and that Peeta had worked the strategy out with Haymitch. She can't bring herself to trust Peeta, despite all the evidence in front of her.

CHAPTERS 16–18

SUMMARY: CHAPTER 16

While Rue sleeps beside her, Katniss considers how to destroy the Careers' supplies and how the Careers' lifetimes of being well-fed will work against them. In the morning, she wakes to the sound of the cannon. Another tribute has died. While Katniss and Rue hunt,

Katniss gets all the information she can out of Rue about the Careers' camp. The food, she learns, is all left in the open, with only one boy guarding it, which sounds suspicious to Katniss. Katniss also learns about Rue. Rue is the oldest of six children, and more than anything she loves music. She sings at work in the orchards, and when the flag is raised to signal the end of the workday, Rue alerts the other workers through a song that she spreads with the mockingjays. By the afternoon, Katniss and Rue have a plan to eliminate the Careers' supplies. While Rue builds three separate campfires to divert the Careers, Katniss will attack the camp. Rue teaches Katniss her song for the mockingjays. There are mockingjays all over the arena, and she says if Katniss hears the song she'll know Rue is okay.

Katniss makes her way to the Careers' camp and hides where she can observe without being seen. There are four tributes, including Cato and a boy from District 3. Most of the supplies sit in a pyramid set at a distance from the camp, and Katniss thinks it must be booby-trapped. Cato shouts to the others and they begin arming themselves. They have seen one of Rue's campfires. They argue about leaving the boy from District 3, and Cato says nobody can get to the supplies anyway so they should take him. Peeta isn't a concern because Cato cut him badly, and even if he's still alive he's in no shape to raid their camp. Katniss waits a long time after they leave before acting. She sees a girl tribute she calls Foxface run out from the woods and carefully pick her path to the supplies, and Katniss realizes the ground is full of landmines. The boy from District 3, Panem's manufacturing hub where even explosives are made, must have planted them. After Foxface leaves, Katniss sees a bag of apples on the pyramid and has an idea. She moves into the open, and with three arrows, she tears the bag open. The apples detonate the mines, and Katniss is blown off her feet in the ensuing explosion.

SUMMARY: CHAPTER 17

Katniss is too dizzy after the blast to walk. She also can't hear out of her left ear. Hiding her fear because she knows the cameras are on her, she crawls as quickly as she can back to her hiding place and gets there just as Cato and the others return. All the supplies have been destroyed, and Cato is furious. He snaps the neck of the boy from District 3. Katniss hides there the whole day. When night falls, the Careers go into the woods in search of whoever blew up their supplies, and Katniss, still recovering, decides to sleep where she is. In the morning, she can hear in her right ear again but her left remains deaf. She sees Foxface scavenging in the remains of the pyramid, but a noise from an ominous-looking area beyond the camp frightens her away.

Katniss heads back to the rendezvous point she established with Rue, but Rue isn't there. Katniss cleans herself up and decides to wait, but after several hours she decides to look for Rue. At the site of the third campfire, she gets the sense that something went wrong. The wood is arranged but was never lit. Katniss hears a mockingjay singing Rue's song, and she follows the trail of song. Suddenly, she hears a girl scream. She takes off running, and as she emerges into a clearing, she finds Rue tangled in a net just as the boy from District 1 stabs her with a spear.

SUMMARY: CHAPTER 18

Katniss immediately shoots the boy from District 1 and kills him. She cuts the net around Rue and sees that Rue is too badly wounded to survive. Rue grasps Katniss's hand and tells her she has to win for them both, then she asks Katniss to sing. Katniss, thinking how much Rue is like Prim, sings a lullaby from her district. Slowly Rue's breathing becomes shallow and finally ceases. While Katniss collects anything useful from Rue and the boy from District 1, feelings of rage toward the Capitol build in her. Thinking of what Peeta once told her, she wants to show the Capitol that Rue was more than just a piece in their game. She covers Rue's body in flowers, and when she's done, she puts her fingers to her lips and holds them out in a gesture of respect used in District 12. For hours after, she walks aimlessly, hoping to bump into the Careers. As she's about to make camp that night, a gift arrives. It's a loaf of bread, the kind Peeta taught her is from District 11. She thinks of the people from District 11 without enough to eat, pooling their money to give her this, and she thanks them aloud.

In the morning, Katniss hardly wants to get up. Only the thought of Prim watching her at home motivates her. She's low on food, so she goes hunting. She thinks of Rue and hopes she'll bump into the other Careers, whom she no longer fears. As the day goes on she replays the events of Rue's death in her head, and she realizes the boy from District 1 is the first person she's deliberately killed in the Games. She thinks of his family and friends at home and their grief and anger. Suddenly trumpets sound, signaling an announcement. Katniss expects a feast, which is a tactic the Gamemakers have used in the past to lure the tributes into the same area for a fight. But instead they announce a rule change. Under the new rule, tributes from the same district will both be declared winners if they are the last two left alive. Katniss, realizing that she and Peeta can both survive, immediately calls out Peeta's name.

ANALYSIS

The inequality between Panem's rich and poor, which had previously been an advantage to the Careers, ironically becomes a vulnerability for Katniss to exploit in this section. The Careers, because they grew up wealthy, have no experience hunting or foraging in the wild, and Katniss thinks the Careers will have a very difficult time feeding themselves without their supplies. Moreover, Katniss thinks their not being accustomed to hunger, as she and Rue are, will also work against them. She notes that the times in the past when non-Career tributes have won the Games have generally been those in which the Careers didn't have a stockpile of supplies to rely on, suggesting that destroying their supplies could provide the advantage Katniss needs to eventually win. The Careers, of course, are aware of how critical their supplies are and defend them. They set mines all around the supply pyramid, but in yet another irony, it is these mines that offer Katniss a means of destroying the pyramid quickly and completely. Had the supplies not been surrounded by mines, Katniss likely would have found it much more difficult, perhaps impossible, to eliminate everything in a single attack.

Rue's death in this section brings to an end the brief sense of security Katniss had begun to feel, leading Katniss to a complete emotional upheaval. With Rue as a companion, Katniss doesn't feel isolated, and for the first time since the Games began she has started to feel relaxed and content. As Katniss and Rue become closer, Katniss starts to treat Rue as a substitute for Prim, her little sister. When Rue wonders how they'll destroy the Careers' supplies, for instance, Katniss pokes Rue in the belly and jokes that maybe they'll eat them, thinking as she does so that she behaves that way with Prim. Katniss abruptly loses this security when Rue dies, and feels devastated as a result. What little serenity she felt turns immediately to rage, leading her to disregard her own safety as she recklessly goes in search of the Careers (this disregard doesn't have any negative consequences since Katniss doesn't encounter anyone). It then turns to despair and depression, and Katniss feels so depressed the next morning that she can hardly force herself to get up and make an effort to survive.

The main force driving Katniss after Rue's death is actually the knowledge that Prim is watching her on television, and indeed through the section Katniss never forgets that the cameras are on her at all times. Even in extraordinarily stressful situations, such as when she's blown up after detonating the mines around the Careers' supplies, Katniss remembers she is being watched and makes it a point not to show fear. Katniss says explicitly that she hides her fear for Prim's sake. She doesn't want her little sister worrying about her, so she tries to remain composed. But she has also suggested earlier in the novel that she considers how the audience and potential sponsors see her as well. In the past, tributes who have appeared weak have been unpopular and have not earned many benefactors, and Katniss realizes letting her emotions show might cost her sponsors, whose gifts could mean the difference between life and death for her. Thus Katniss's awareness of the cameras and her unshakable composure act as part of her survival strategy.

Katniss's decorating Rue's body is an act of defiance against the Capitol, and it recalls Peeta's desire to show the Capitol he's not just a pawn in their game. The Hunger Games, by their nature, dehumanize the tributes. They essentially objectify them, turning them into commodities rather than recognizing them as people, so that the audience at home feels entertained by their deaths rather than horrified. In the lead-up to the Games, for instance, the tributes are expected to be cheerful and not show how fearful and anxious they may be. As a result, the audience never experiences them as real people, but more as characters playing roles. (The talk show–like treatment of each tribute's backstory leading up to the Games similarly treats them more as characters than real people and increases their entertainment value.) The tributes are, of course, aware of how they're being objectified. But when Katniss decorates Rue's body and openly grieves for her, it forces the audience to remember Rue and realize how painful her death is for those who knew and loved her. By doing so, Katniss humanizes Rue and does for her what Peeta had hoped to do for himself.

In this section, Katniss deliberately kills someone for the first time in the Hunger Games and suffers the emotional consequences that result. The two prior deaths that resulted from Katniss's actions, those of Glimmer and another girl when Katniss dropped the tracker jacker nest, were not entirely intended. Katniss's foremost concern was escaping, and dropping the nest on the tributes below was the best means she had of doing that. She also didn't kill them directly. But when Katniss kills the boy who stabs Rue, she intends to kill him and is directly responsible for his death. Consequently, she also feels more responsible. Though she is still mourning Rue, she finds herself thinking about the boy, wondering about his family's grief, his friends' anger, and if he had a girlfriend who was hoping he would return home. Though Katniss is an experienced hunter, she clearly feels uncomfortable at the thought of having killed him. This discomfort lasts only briefly, however, as she remembers Rue's death and pushes the boy out of her mind, suggesting she feels justified in having killed him.

By this point in the book, mockingjays have become a prominent motif, and in this section they take on their most notable role yet. The birds have been repeatedly mentioned throughout the novel but have thus far remained mostly in the background. But the mockingjay motif becomes more significant as Katniss allies with Rue. The bird, as Katniss explained earlier, is a subtle symbol of rebellion since it represents a failure by the Capitol. But after Rue explains how she and the other workers in District 11 use the mockingjays to communicate, the mockingjay takes on an additional role. Katniss and Rue decide to use the birds as a way to communicate with one another. That role lasts only briefly as Rue is killed, but Katniss hears the mockingjays still singing Rue's song, and the birds essentially become a reminder of Rue as well.

CHAPTERS 19–21

SUMMARY: CHAPTER 19

Katniss thinks of Peeta's behavior before and during the Games. She realizes the feelings he's expressed for her have given an advantage to them both. Before going to sleep for the night, she thinks of the remaining tributes and decides the real threats are Cato and the girl from his district. In the morning, Katniss looks for Peeta. She knows he needs water to survive, so she follows the stream until suddenly she hears him calling. He is lying on the ground, camouflaged in mud. Peeta's skill frosting cakes has paid off, but his leg is badly cut, and he can barely move. With great difficulty and care, Katniss cleans him up, stripping off most of his mud-caked clothing, and treats the infected wound as best she can. They need to move, but Peeta can't walk, so Katniss helps him to a cave where he'll be hidden. Peeta starts telling her what to do if he doesn't survive, but Katniss tells him not to talk like that. She kisses him, thinking of how they're supposed to be in love. She steps outside, and a new gift from Haymitch arrives. It's a pot of hot broth, and Katniss realizes Haymitch wants her to play up the romance.

SUMMARY: CHAPTER 20

Katniss spends the night caring for Peeta, who is feverish because of the infection. In the morning, he keeps trying to be playfully romantic, but Katniss won't play along. Later that day, Katniss sees that Peeta's leg is getting worse. The infection is spreading. When Katniss returns from gathering food, Peeta asks her to tell him a story, and Katniss tells the story of how she got Prim a goat. Because she doesn't want to get other people in trouble by connecting them with her illegal hunting, she says she got the money for the goat by selling her mother's old silver locket, but in reality she and Gale killed a large buck and sold it at the Hob. On Prim's birthday, Katniss went back to the Hob to buy dress materials, when she saw an old disabled man selling a goat that had been mauled by a dog. The goat was to be sold to the butcher, but the butcher said she no longer wanted it. Katniss haggled with the old man. If the goat lived, she was getting a great deal, but if it died she would have thrown away her money. She ended up taking the goat. Prim fell in love with it immediately, and she and her mother were able to treat its injury and save it. Katniss says the goat more than repaid the cost of saving it, and Peeta says one day he'll do the same.

The trumpets sound, and the announcer, Claudius Templesmith, declares that there will be a feast. Katniss isn't interested at first, but Claudius Templesmith says there will be a backpack waiting for each person containing something they desperately need. Before Katniss can speak, Peeta says he doesn't want her to risk her life for him. They argue, with Peeta swearing he'll follow her if she goes. Katniss heads down to the stream to wash up, and while she's thinking that Peeta won't survive without medicine, a new gift arrives from Haymitch. But it's not the medicine she needs. It's sleep syrup, commonly used in the districts, and Katniss realizes it will knock Peeta out long enough for her to go to the feast. Katniss mashes some berries and mixes the syrup in. She goes back to Peeta and tells him she has a treat for him. He recognizes the flavor of the overly sweet sleep syrup too late, and after a moment he is completely unconscious.

SUMMARY: CHAPTER 21

While waiting for the feast at dawn, Katniss thinks about the people in District 12 watching the Games. She wonders if Gale wants Peeta to survive, and if he has any romantic interest in her. Thinking of the audience at home, she gives Peeta a lingering kiss and pretends to brush away a tear before she leaves. She makes it back to the Cornucopia, where the feast will be, and just as the sun rises, a table comes up out of the ground with a few backpacks and one tiny pack that Katniss assumes must be for her. Foxface runs out of the Cornucopia immediately and grabs the backpack meant for her before anyone else reacts. Wishing she had done the same, Katniss sprints to the table, and just as she gets to her backpack, a knife clips her forehead, spilling blood down her face. Clove, the girl tribute from District 2, slams into her, knocking her down. Clove pins her, taunting her all the while, and says they're going to kill her like they did her ally, Rue.

But just as Clove cuts Katniss's lip, Thresh, the boy from District 11, grabs Clove. He asks her if she cut up Rue like she was going to cut Katniss, and he crushes her skull with a rock. He turns to Katniss and asks what Clove meant, calling her Rue's ally. When Katniss explains, he says he'll let her live, but now they're even. As Katniss runs off, she turns to see Thresh running away with two large backpacks and Cato kneeling beside Clove's body. Katniss doesn't stop running until she reaches the stream. She's terrified and dazed from her wound, but she suspects Cato will pursue Thresh, not her, since Thresh took the backpack meant for him. She makes her way back to the cave and crawls in, then dumps the contents of the small pack. It's a hypodermic needle, which she injects into Peeta's arm. A few moments later she passes out.

ANALYSIS

The intimacy between Katniss and Peeta increases dramatically in this section. Because Peeta is so severely injured, he is unable to care for himself. Katniss becomes his caregiver, treating his wounds, feeding him, and even telling him a story to soothe him. Through her actions, Katniss reveals how much she cares for Peeta, and the emotional intimacy between them, which had waned before they entered the arena, reaches a new level. Moreover, Katniss must also remove all his mud-covered clothing, creating a physical intimacy between them that they had never experienced before. This physical intimacy only increases throughout the section as Katniss and Peeta share their first kiss, and later in the section, share a sleeping bag for the night. As a result, their friendship, which had previously verged on the romantic because of Peeta's honesty about his feelings for Katniss, essentially leaves the realm of friendship and does finally become romantic, even if Katniss's feelings are mixed.

Notably, when Katniss kisses Peeta, it is clear that she does it for the cameras rather than out of a genuine romantic interest in Peeta, and internally she still feels conflicted about him. Katniss thinks about how she and Peeta are supposed to be in love as she kisses him, and she also points out that she realizes Peeta's feelings have actually been to her benefit. Their relationship has attracted a great deal of attention, which in turn means more sponsors. Haymitch has continually reminded her of this trade-off, and Katniss at times exploits this leverage, even pretending to wipe away a tear as she prepares to leave for the feast. But Katniss clearly feels ambivalent about her relationship with Peeta. When Peeta keeps behaving affectionately toward her as she nurses him back to health, for instance, Katniss appears uncomfortable. Moreover, Katniss thinks about Gale and wonders how he is taking her intimacy with Peeta. Though she and Gale don't have a romantic relationship, she wonders if Gale would be open to the idea, suggesting that what romantic feelings she has lie with him. Katniss, however, feels compelled to keep up the pretense of romance with Peeta because of the strategic advantage it provides, whether she's romantically interested in Peeta or not.

The story Katniss tells Peeta to soothe him actually offers a good summation of everything that makes Katniss feel good. Peeta doesn't ask Katniss for a specific story, so that Katniss's choice of this story suggests that it is what would make her feel better. The story starts with Katniss and Gale hunting together, though she doesn't mention this part to Peeta. From Katniss's previous descriptions of her time spent with Gale, it's clear that she enjoys his company, and being in the woods with him is the only time she feels she can be completely herself. The day she describes is a particularly successful one. They take down a large buck that Katniss knows will fetch a good price at the Hob, a detail that Katniss remembers with a sense of pride, and the buck brings them more money than they're accustomed to. For Katniss, who acts as the provider in her family, this trade means both that she will be able to feed her family and she'll have money left over to buy Prim a present for her birthday. Katniss, using her wits, is then able to buy a goat, which further helps her provide for her family. But more important, as Peeta points out, it brings Prim a great deal of joy, and from her story it is clear that Katniss counts making Prim so happy among her top achievements. Katniss's mother, meanwhile, is notably absent from the story, suggesting she is not someone who generally makes Katniss feel good.

The feast called by Claudius Templesmith creates a new set of dramatic conflicts for Katniss. Katniss knows the Gamemakers have called the feast as a way to bring the remaining tributes together with the goal of drawing them all into a fight. Going to the feast could potentially mean her death, and initially she waves off the idea of going. But when Claudius Templesmith announces that the tributes of each district will get something they desperately need, Katniss is faced with a difficult problem. Peeta's wound is badly infected, and she knows without proper medicine he will die. It seems likely that the item at the feast for District 12 will be the medicine Peeta needs, leaving Katniss with a difficult choice: She can go to the feast, which will put her life at risk but could save Peeta's if she survives, or she can avoid the feast, keeping her safe but meaning Peeta's certain death. Peeta protests and says he'll follow her, and Katniss, knowing it's his only chance of survival, ultimately decides to drug him and go to the feast, demonstrating her courage and her sense of loyalty to Peeta.

At the feast, Katniss, who has previously managed to avoid any direct fights, barely escapes alive from her first real battle with another tribute, and what ultimately saves her is her compassion, something she had previously thought a liability. Earlier in the Games, Katniss had fought other tributes indirectly, as when she dropped the tracker jacker nest on the tributes waiting at the base of the tree she was in, or she struck from a distance, as when she killed the boy who stabbed Rue. Here, however, Katniss ends up in a hand-to-hand fight with Clove, and she essentially loses the fight. Clove has her pinned, and it is only because Clove takes too long taunting Katniss (a trope common in commercial action movies) that she isn't able to kill Katniss. Thresh, the boy who came with Rue from District 11, pulls Clove off and kills her by smashing her head with a rock. The scene marks the first time Katniss has been in immediate danger of dying, as well as the first time that Katniss's abilities and resourcefulness fail her. What prevents Thresh from killing her is the friendship she had with Rue and the way she mourned Rue's death, or in other words, her compassion toward Rue. Ironically, it was this sort of compassion that Katniss thought might get her killed when she and Peeta began to develop a friendship. Rather than hamper her, however, it proves advantageous.

CHAPTERS 22–24

SUMMARY: CHAPTER 22

Katniss wakes after a long sleep to find Peeta recuperated. It's raining hard outside so Peeta has arranged everything to keep them dry. Katniss feels weak from the wound on her head. She tells Peeta what happened at the feast and about Rue. She says Thresh was paying back a debt in letting her live, but Peeta wouldn't understand because he's not poor. Katniss says it's like the bread he gave her and how she can never pay him back. She asks why he did that, and Peeta responds that she knows why. They talk about Cato and Thresh. Katniss feels upset, thinking she's tired of the Games. She doesn't want anyone else to die. She begins to cry and says she wants to go home.

Later, while they eat the last of the food, Katniss asks if Peeta knows what's on the far side of the circle where the Cornucopia is, where Thresh stays. Peeta says it's a field of shoulder-high grass. It makes him uneasy thinking about what can hide in there. Peeta's description reminds Katniss of what they're taught about the woods outside District 12, and she compares Peeta to Gale. While Peeta is not a coward, there are things he's never questioned, like what the woods are really like. Gale questions everything. Katniss makes a joke about knocking Peeta out, and when Peeta becomes genuinely upset that she risked her life, she decides to use the romantic tension between them in the hopes of getting more gifts from Haymitch. But as she does this, she realizes she truly cares for Peeta. When they kiss, Katniss describes it as the first that both are fully aware of. Neither is sick or dazed by injury, and it's the first kiss that makes her want another. Because of the cold, they share the sleeping bag again, and Peeta puts his arms around her. It's the closest she's ever felt to him, and nobody has made her feel so safe since her father died.

The weather is so bad the next day that they can't go outside. Katniss knows they need food, but Haymitch isn't sending any, so she wonders how she can ramp up the romance with Peeta. She asks him how long he's had a crush on her, and he says since their first day of school. His father pointed her out and told Peeta he had wanted to marry Katniss's mother, but she ran off with a coal miner who sang so well even the birds would stop and listen. When their teacher asked if anyone knew the valley song, Katniss raised her hand and sang it for the class. Peeta fell in love and had been unsuccessfully trying to talk to her ever since. The story makes Katniss feel suddenly confused. Their romance was supposed to be a fiction, but Katniss is beginning to feel it's real. Peeta jokes that she pays attention to him now because he has no competition there, and Katniss, thinking of what Haymitch would want her to say, says he has no competition anywhere. As they go to kiss, there's a noise outside. It's a basket of food from Haymitch.

SUMMARY: CHAPTER 23

Unable to leave, Katniss and Peeta lie together and talk. Peeta points out that if they make it back, Katniss won't be a girl from the Seam anymore. People who win the Hunger Games are set up with houses in a separate section of the district called the Victor's Village. Haymitch would be their only neighbor. They make a few jokes about him, and Katniss notices that he ignores Peeta and only communicates with her because she understands what he wants to see. They wonder how Haymitch won the Hunger Games, and Peeta guesses he must have outsmarted the other tributes. That night, Thresh's picture is projected in the sky. Thresh is dead, and the news upsets Katniss. If they didn't win, she wanted Thresh to, because he let her live and because of Rue. Only Foxface and Cato remain. Katniss and Peeta sleep in shifts, and when Peeta wakes Katniss he offers her some bread with goat cheese and apples. They make tarts like those at his family's bakery, tarts they can't afford to eat at home. Peeta's family mostly eats the stale leftovers. Katniss is surprised. She always thought the shopkeepers had everything.

While Katniss keeps watch, she thinks of what it would be like to win the Games. Her family would have all they need, and she wonders how not having to provide for them would change her identity. By morning, the rain has stopped, and they decide to hunt. They walk back to Katniss's old hunting grounds, but Peeta with his wounded leg is so loud he chases off any game nearby. They walk for hours without catching anything, so Peeta suggests they split up. Katniss shows Peeta edible roots to gather and goes to hunt. After catching some rabbits and a squirrel, she heads back toward Peeta. They've been whistling back and forth to communicate. But she hasn't heard him for some time, and she begins to panic when he doesn't respond to her whistling now. Where they split up she finds a pile of roots and some berries laid out on a tarp. He returns, explaining he was down by the stream collecting berries. While Katniss reprimands him, she notices some of their food has been eaten, and looking more closely at the berries she recognizes them as nightlock. The cannon sounds just before a hovercraft appears to take Foxface's body. Peeta thinks Cato is near, but Katniss tells Peeta he's the one who killed her and holds out the berries he collected.

SUMMARY: CHAPTER 24

Katniss explains that the berries, some of which Foxface stole, are poisonous. In a way, Peeta outsmarted Foxface. They decide to hold on to the rest of the berries in case the same opportunity arises with Cato. Cato must know where they are now, so they cook their food and then head back to the cave they've been staying in. The night passes without any trouble, and when they leave the cave in the morning Katniss suspects it will be her last night in the arena. The Gamemakers will find a way to push Katniss, Peeta, and Cato together, and when they reach the stream, it's totally dry. The Gamemakers have drained it. Every water source they check is the same, and they realize if they want water they'll have to go to the lake by the Cornucopia.

They're cautious arriving at the lake, but there's no sign of Cato. As they sit in the open, waiting, Katniss sings Rue's song to the mockingjays she sees. They sing back pleasantly, until suddenly their song breaks up. Cato comes sprinting out of the trees with no weapons, and it's clear he's been running hard for a long time. Katniss hits him directly in the chest with an arrow, but he's wearing some form of body armor and the arrow bounces harmlessly away. Katniss prepares for impact, but Cato runs directly between Peeta and her. Katniss, seeing strange creatures approaching in the distance, turns and runs.

ANALYSIS

Much of the action in this section centers on Katniss and Peeta simply talking, which dramatically increases the sense of intimacy between them. Because of the rain, they are unable to leave the cave, and consequently they have far more time to speak privately (albeit with cameras broadcasting their conversations) than they generally have in the past. The result is that they are more honest with one another than at any time before. Katniss, for instance, finds out that Peeta's feelings for her date all the way back to their first day of school together. He remembers the day in great detail, recalling everything about Katniss down to the dress she was wearing and how her hair was done, and he reveals that his father was once in love with Katniss's mother. Katniss, for the first time, tells Peeta how she still feels indebted to him for the bread he gave her years earlier, and she tells Peeta everything that happened with Rue. Their honesty with one another not only brings them closer, it causes Katniss to recognize that Peeta's feelings for her are genuine and not part of a strategy he devised with Haymitch.

For the first time in the novel, Katniss, who has always maintained a stoic front, feels overwhelmed by her emotions to the point that she's unable to control them. When Peeta and Katniss talk about Thresh, Katniss notes that under different circumstances they might be friends with Thresh, essentially recognizing him as an individual rather than just a competitor. When Peeta hopes that Cato will kill Thresh so they don't have to, she thinks that she doesn't want anyone to die, and she is unable to restrain the tears from welling up in her eyes. Prior to this point, she has always been capable of keeping her feelings in check, or at least not letting them show outwardly, particularly when she thinks of Prim watching her. Now, however, she compares herself to a small child, suggesting she feels weak, vulnerable, and incapable of controlling the situation. When Thresh comes up again in conversation later, Katniss has a similar reaction. She hugs herself tightly as if to protect herself, again suggesting feelings of vulnerability, and she pulls her hood over her face so that the cameras can't see her reaction. Moreover, her use of the term *murder* to describe Thresh's death implies that it's the injustice of his death that provokes this response in her.

While Katniss has felt generally ambivalent toward Peeta, she begins to reciprocate his feelings while the two are stuck inside during the thunderstorm. What seems to trigger this change in Katniss is her realization—or perhaps acceptance, since she seemed to suspect Peeta's feelings were genuine but didn't want to admit it—that Peeta's romantic interest in her is real and not just a strategy he and Haymitch devised. She comes to this realization gradually, starting at the moment when they have what she describes as the first kiss they're both fully aware of, meaning neither was sick or dazed by an injury at the time. Katniss says the kiss stirs something in her, and it's the first that makes her want another. Later, Peeta dispels whatever doubts Katniss has about whether his feelings for her are real when he provides several details about how she looked and behaved on their first day of school, when he says his crush on her began, proving that he was paying attention to her long before he was selected as a tribute. Katniss thinks they're supposed to be acting as though they're in love, not actually being in love, implying that she feels something for Peeta as well.

Though Katniss begins to develop genuine feelings for Peeta, the affection she shows him almost always has an ulterior motive: to please Haymitch and elicit presents from him. Katniss has previously realized that she can get gifts from sponsors through Haymitch if she plays up her romance with Peeta, and these gifts can be critical to Katniss and Peeta's survival. As a result, in almost every instance in which she and Peeta are behaving affectionately, either through kissing or in the way they're speaking, Katniss is thinking of what Haymitch would want to see. Katniss, for instance, provokes the conversation about when Peeta's crush on her started because she thinks Haymitch is looking for something more personal than kissing. Even as Katniss realizes she's developing genuine feelings for Peeta, her thoughts about what Haymitch wants guide her. When Peeta jokes that Katniss is only paying attention to him now because they're in the arena, where he has no competition, Katniss thinks first of what Haymitch would want her to say before replying that he has no competition anywhere. Katniss and Peeta then promptly receive a basket of food containing a lamb stew that Katniss said she liked in her interview with Caesar Flickerman, indicating that Haymitch is rewarding her in particular.

Various issues centering on wealth and poverty also appear in this section. Katniss is surprised to learn that Peeta's family can't afford to eat some of the goods they sell at his family's bakery, and this knowledge forces her to rethink her view of Peeta's life. She thinks that even though Peeta always has enough to eat it must be depressing to live off of the stale leftovers nobody else wants, and when she thinks that at least her family's food is fresh, it suggests she feels that, at least in this one regard, her life is actually better than Peeta's. Wealth turns up again in Katniss's thoughts as she thinks what life would be like if she won the Games. She realizes her family would have everything it needs, meaning she would no longer have to provide for them. Rather than bringing her a sense of relief, however, the thought makes her uncomfortable. Katniss defines herself in large part by the role she plays as the provider in her family, and losing that role means losing a significant part of her identity.

Peeta's lack of experience foraging for his own food ironically benefits him and Katniss when he indirectly causes Foxface's death with the poisonous berries he collects. Throughout the Hunger Games, knowing how to find food in the forest has proved one of the greatest advantages a tribute could have. It provided Katniss, as well as Rue and probably Thresh, with a distinct advantage over the Career Tributes. Peeta, of course, did not share this advantage. As the son of a baker, he had no experience providing his own food, and he even jokes that he's essentially of no use to Katniss unless they happen to find a bread bush. Katniss regards this lack of survival skills as a hindrance, and coupled with Peeta's injured leg, which makes him so loud he scares away all the game, Katniss begins to think Peeta's presence is a liability. When she sees that the poisonous berries he collected killed Foxface, however, she thinks that his inexperience was actually a good thing. Foxface, whom Katniss considers the most intelligent of the tributes, would likely have recognized a deliberate trap. She didn't sense a trap because Peeta was genuinely ignorant, and so they inadvertently managed to eliminate one more competitor in the Games.

CHAPTERS 25–27

SUMMARY: CHAPTER 25

Katniss recognizes the strange creatures chasing Cato as muttations, hybrid animals engineered by the Capitol. These muttations look like giant wolves but can walk upright like humans. Cato runs to the Cornucopia and Katniss follows, but she realizes Peeta can't keep up because of his injured leg. Unable to help him from the ground, she climbs to the top of the Cornucopia and fires arrows at the approaching muttations, allowing Peeta to climb up just in time to escape them. When one muttation jumps to reach them, Katniss realizes it's Glimmer. The dead tributes have been turned into these creatures. One jumps high enough to grab Peeta, and Katniss just gets hold of him before he's pulled over the side. He gets free, but when Katniss thinks he's safe, Cato begins strangling him in a headlock. Cato threatens that if Katniss shoots him, Peeta will go over the side too. Peeta reaches to the gash the muttation left in his leg and draws an "X" in blood on Cato's hand. Cato realizes what he's doing just as Katniss shoots him, and when he lets go Peeta shoves him to the ground below.

Cato, in his body armor, fights the muttations off for an hour before he is dragged into the Cornucopia. Night falls, and still no cannon announces his death. They can hear Cato moaning as the muttations work away at him, but Katniss knows they won't kill him. The Gamemakers want to prolong the gruesome spectacle for the viewers. Peeta, meanwhile, is bleeding heavily from the wound in his leg, which Katniss has tied with a tourniquet. When morning comes, Katniss realizes Peeta won't survive much longer. She climbs down over the ledge and sees Cato, mutilated but alive. Out of pity as much as to win, she kills him. The cannon sounds and the muttations leave, but still the Games don't end. Katniss and Peeta climb down but just as Katniss thinks they've won, Claudius Templesmith announces that the previous rule change has been revoked: There can now be only one winner again. Peeta says he isn't surprised, and as he draws his knife Katniss takes aim at him. Peeta tells her to shoot, but she can't. Then, realizing the Gamemakers won't allow both of them to die, she has an idea. She takes the poisonous berries from her pouch. As Katniss and Peeta pop the berries into their mouths, Claudius Templesmith shouts for them to stop and announces that they are both the winners of the Seventy-Fourth Hunger Games.

SUMMARY: CHAPTER 26

They spit out the berries, and shortly after they're lifted into a hovercraft. Doctors go to work on Peeta immediately and Katniss is dragged to a separate room where she's given a glass of orange juice. She catches her reflection in the room's glass door and hardly recognizes the feral, crazed-looking person she's become. After a time they land back at the Training Center. Katniss has a violent fit when she sees them taking Peeta away, until a needle jabs her and she falls unconscious. She wakes in a different room and finds herself clean and healed. She can even hear out of her left ear again. The redheaded Avox comes in to feed her, and when Katniss asks if Peeta made it, she nods that he did. Katniss is kept restrained to her bed in this room for an indeterminate amount of time, possibly days.

Eventually she wakes up and finds her restraint gone. An outfit, the same one the tributes wore into the arena, is set out for her at the end of her bed. In the hall, she sees Effie, Haymitch, and Cinna. She runs first to Haymitch, who hugs her and tells her she did a good job, then Cinna embraces her. Her reunion with Peeta will be at the closing ceremony, and they take her to be prepped and dressed. Cinna puts her in a simple dress that recalls candlelight and makes her look young and innocent. He says Peeta will like it, but Katniss knows Cinna has some other reason that has to do with the

Capitol. She is taken to a waiting area under the stage where she meets Haymitch. He says she looks good enough and asks for a hug, but when Katniss hugs him he doesn't let her go. He tells her she's in danger. The Capitol is furious at her showing them up in the arena. Her only defense can be that she was madly in love with Peeta. As she prepares to be raised up to the stage for her interview, she feels terrified that she, Peeta, and even their families may be in danger.

SUMMARY: CHAPTER 27

After the District 12 team, including Effie, the stylists, and Haymitch, is introduced, Katniss is raised up to the stage. When she sees Peeta she runs to him, knocking him slightly off balance, and she realizes he has a cane. They embrace for a long time before they're seated together on a love seat. Katniss, taking a cue from Haymitch, puts her head on Peeta's shoulder. They watch a reel of highlights from the Games, and after it ends President Snow places a crown on Peeta and another on Katniss. Though President Snow is smiling, Katniss can see he's unhappy with her. When the event is over they go to the president's mansion for the Victory Banquet, then back to the Training Center. Katniss wants to talk to Peeta privately, but Haymitch won't let her. That night, she sneaks out of her room and looks for Peeta but can't find him. She returns to her room, and when she decides to go straight to his room, she finds her door has been locked from the outside.

The next day she and Peeta are interviewed by Caesar Flickerman. Katniss is nervous because she has to be very careful what she says. She stumbles over her words when Caesar Flickerman asks when she realized she was in love with Peeta, until Caesar suggests it was when she called out Peeta's name to find him. Katniss shrewdly replies that prior to that she didn't want to have feelings for him, but that's when she knew she could keep him. Caesar asks Peeta how his new leg is, and Katniss learns that Peeta now has a prosthetic leg. Finally, Caesar asks Katniss what was going through her mind when she pulled out the berries. Katniss realizes this moment is critical: she can frame the decision as a rebellion against the Capitol or as an act of desperation at the thought of losing Peeta, and she says she couldn't bear the thought of losing Peeta. Haymitch tells her later that she was perfect.

On the train back to District 12, Katniss thinks of her family and Gale. During a refueling stop, Haymitch tells Katniss to keep it up in the district until the cameras are gone. Peeta doesn't know what

Haymitch is talking about, and Katniss explains that the Capitol is unhappy about the stunt with the berries and that Haymitch has been coaching her. Peeta angrily asks if Katniss has been acting the whole time. She says not everything has been an act, but the closer they get to home the more confused she becomes. As Peeta walks off she wants to explain that she can't fully love him or anyone else after what they've been through, but she doesn't. The train arrives in District 12, where a crowd of cameras awaits on the platform. Peeta takes her hand, saying they'll pretend one more time, and Katniss fears the moment when she'll finally have to let go.

Analysis

The theme of suffering as entertainment reaches its greatest extreme in Cato's slow death at the Cornucopia. The real-life suffering of the tributes is essentially what makes the Hunger Games entertaining to watch, much like the real deaths of the gladiators made the gladiatorial games entertaining to the Roman populace. The finale of the Games, being ideally the most dramatic and entertaining part, should therefore entail the most suffering. Katniss comments on this fact as she and Peeta wait for Cato to die after he is knocked off the Cornucopia. She realizes the Gamemakers won't simply have the muttations kill Cato because prolonging his agony increases the drama of the finale. When Katniss climbs over the ledge and sees him, she describes him as looking like a "raw hunk of meat," indicating that he has been savagely mauled and undoubtedly is in intense pain. By this point, Cato no longer has any chance of surviving, and it's clear that the Gamemakers haven't ended the competition because of the entertainment value of the grotesque spectacle.

The muttations play a central role in making the finale grotesque and dramatic, as being turned into savage hybrid animals is the ultimate form of dehumanization for the tributes. Throughout the Games, the Capitol has treated the tributes as commodities whose foremost purpose is to entertain the viewers at home. In other words, the Capitol turns them into objects and dismisses their humanity and individuality. Here, the Capitol literally dehumanizes the dead tributes, turning them into vicious wolflike creatures. These tribute muttations are vicious, strong, and fast, but they're most horrifying to Katniss, and presumably fascinating to the viewers at home, because they retain some of the physical characteristics of their human selves, allowing them to be recognized. Their former personalities, however, are completely stripped away and replaced by a single-minded drive to kill Katniss, Peeta, and Cato. In this way they've become the perfect tool for the Capitol: they are both a new danger for the living tributes to overcome and they are in themselves a spectacle to amuse the viewers at home.

The Gamemakers try to make the finale yet more "entertaining" by announcing that there can only be one winner again. Katniss realizes the Gamemakers never intended to let both of them survive, suggesting they wanted to manufacture a dramatic fight to the death between the two. The scenario would, of course, be exceedingly awful for two tributes who are supposed to be in love, but ostensibly it would be great entertainment for the viewers. This intent is thwarted, however, by Katniss's idea for the two of them to eat the berries. The book never makes it entirely clear why their suicide would be more objectionable to the viewers than having them fight each other to the death. But it suggests that, had Katniss and Peeta actually carried out their suicides, the Games would have been deeply upsetting to the viewers at home. The suffering that was supposed to provide entertainment would have become too emotionally charged as a result, turning the Games from amusement to a real-life tragedy.

Katniss performs the novel's greatest act of rebellion against the Capitol when she has the idea that they should eat the poisonous berries. As Katniss explains, the Hunger Games are the Capitol's weapon against the districts, but they are also a popular form of entertainment. But having the two finalists, who are supposedly madly in love, commit suicide would be extremely unpopular among the viewers, and therefore potentially troublesome for the Capitol. Thus Katniss's idea with the berries essentially turns the Capitol's weapon back on itself. The Capitol's concession of allowing two Hunger Games winners after declaring there would only be one makes the Capitol look weak, however. More specifically, it makes them look as if they've lost control. Since the Capitol needs to keep strict control over its populace to maintain the status quo, this defeat, the story suggests, could ultimately cause problems, though it's never stated exactly what these problems might be. Katniss, as a result of her rebellion and the problems it may cause, becomes a target of the Capitol.

Because of Katniss's defiance of the Capitol, appearances become perhaps more important than ever in the novel. The Capitol is furious with Katniss for her power play with the berries, which was essentially an outright rebellion against the Capitol's declaration that there would be one winner of the Hunger Games. The only defense that will allow Katniss to avoid the Capitol's retribution is that she was so in love with Peeta she couldn't bear to be without him. In other words, she needs to make her defiance look like an act of love and not rebellion. This need to frame her behavior as love motivates essentially everything she says and does, notably laying her head on Peeta in her interview with Caesar Flickerman after the Games. Cinna is aware of this need as well, and knowing that Katniss's physical appearance will affect how the audience and the Capitol feel about her, he designs a dress for her that makes her appear young and innocent. Ultimately, every public appearance Katniss makes after the Games requires her to maintain the fiction that she's completely in love with Peeta. Failing to do so could put Katniss and her family, as well as Peeta and even his family, in danger.

The contrast between Katniss and the pristine conditions she encounters in the hovercraft after being taken from the arena, and later back in the Training Center, highlight how brutal the Hunger Games have been on her. When Katniss is given the glass of orange juice after being dragged to a room in the hovercraft, she immediately notices the incongruity between the clean, crystal glass filled with cold juice and a straw with a "frilly" collar, and her filthy, bloody hand. The cold orange juice, obtained so easily here, stands in stark contrast with Katniss's experience of the past weeks, during which she has had to work for all her food and fight just to stay alive. In the arena she left moments earlier, orange juice would have been a luxury (it would also be considered a luxury in District 12). The frilly collar on the straw specifically suggests a particularly extravagant and indeed needless luxury. Katniss's appearance, meanwhile, represents all the hardships she has endured during the Games. She is unwashed, bloody from the injuries she's sustained, and as she notices in the Training Center, extremely thin from lack of food coupled with hard exertion. This same contrast persists as Katniss rehabilitates in the comfort of the Training Center, and throughout the section it essentially symbolizes the power of the Capitol, with its ability to reduce Katniss to her present condition or grant her luxuries however it chooses.

As the book draws to a close, Katniss still feels ambivalent about Peeta. While she cares for Peeta and doesn't want to lose him, she doesn't love him in the way that he loves her. Though she has developed a romantic interest in him, her feelings toward him have always been tentative, even after she realized that his feelings for her were genuine. Moreover, Katniss still feels torn between her interest in Peeta and her interest in Gale. She feels more comfortable with Gale than she does with anyone else, and as she returns home to District 12, she wonders whether her relationship with Gale could turn from friendship to romance. Finally, in the aftermath of the Hunger Games, given the horrible experiences she's endured, she's not certain she can love anyone fully enough to marry and start a family. (Perhaps it's a premature concern given that Katniss is just sixteen, but it's a concern for her nonetheless.) The dramatic tension in the book's final line centers on Katniss's ambivalence toward Peeta. Though she may not feel for him as he does for her, she acknowledges that she still fears the moment she'll have to let him go.

Important Quotations Explained

1. "I volunteer!" I gasp. "I volunteer as tribute!"

At the outset of Chapter 2, just after Prim has been selected in the reaping, Katniss volunteers to serve as the female tribute for District 12 in the Hunger Games. This event sets the rest of the plot in motion, and for the remainder of the book we watch Katniss struggling to survive the Games. The reason Katniss volunteers is, of course, to save Prim, her little sister. Despite the odds being in her favor, Prim is selected by the lottery system that decides which children become tributes. Because she is just twelve years old, and because she is a sensitive, nurturing person who has difficulty with any kind of suffering or violence, she is almost certain to die in the Games. Katniss, meanwhile, is four years older and very protective of Prim, and so without hesitation she volunteers to take her sister's place. Moreover, she has years of experience hunting (and therefore killing) and is much tougher than her sister, making her more likely to survive the ordeal of the Games.

Katniss's volunteering is also notable because, as Katniss explains, volunteers in her district are basically unheard of. Tributes from poor districts, such as Katniss's District 12, rarely win the Games because their poverty puts them at a distinct disadvantage. They are often malnourished compared to the children from the wealthier districts, making them weaker and less able to endure prolonged exertion and difficult conditions. Additionally, as we learn later, some children in the wealthy districts actually train their whole lives to take part in the Hunger Games. Volunteers in these districts are common because winning the Games is a great honor for them. But because the tributes from the poor areas are vastly more likely to be killed, it is exceedingly rare that someone volunteers, even apparently to take the place of a sibling. Katniss's gesture instantly earns the respect of her district and makes her unusual among the tributes in the Hunger Games.

2. The boy took one look back to the bakery as if checking that the coast was clear, then, his attention back on the pig, he threw a loaf of bread in my direction. The second quickly followed, and he sloshed back to the bakery, closing the kitchen door tightly behind him.

This quotation occurs toward the end of Chapter 2, after Peeta has been selected as District 12's male tribute. Katniss relates her first encounter with him. Katniss credits Peeta's actions with essentially saving her life at the time and helping her realize that she will have to act as the provider for her family. When Peeta gave Katniss the bread, Katniss and her family were basically starving. The bread Peeta gave her allowed them to have their first real meal in a long while, and when Katniss saw Peeta the next day at the same time she saw the dandelion in the schoolyard, she realized that, if she wanted her family to eat, she would have to hunt and forage as her father taught her. Since then, Katniss has associated Peeta with this realization.

The quote and the events leading up to it lay the groundwork for the relationship Peeta and Katniss will later develop, and they foreshadow how Peeta acts in the arena. Just before Peeta gives Katniss the bread, Katniss hears some sort of commotion in the bakery and she notices that Peeta emerges with a welt on his cheek, suggesting his mother hit him. Katniss suspects she hit Peeta because he burned the bread, and she also suspects he burned the bread deliberately so that it would be considered damaged and he could give it to Katniss. In other words, Peeta endures a physical beating so that he can help Katniss. He does the same later in the Hunger Games, when he saves Katniss after she's dropped the tracker jacker nest on the group of Career Tributes. When Peeta finds Katniss stunned from the tracker jacker stings, he allows her to run away and he fights Cato to protect her, suffering a serious injury in the process.

3. "I want the audience to recognize you when you're in the arena," says Cinna dreamily. "Katniss, the girl who was on fire."

Cinna says these words to Katniss in Chapter 5 as he prepares her dress for the opening ceremony of the Hunger Games. The quote points to one of the main themes of the novel: the importance of appearances. Cinna understands how necessary it is to make Katniss stand out, not just for the sake of vanity, but because he knows that appearances in the Hunger Games can have a significant, tangible effect. By standing out during the ceremony, for instance, Katniss can attract fans who might not otherwise have noticed her, and among these fans may be sponsors who can provide gifts that might prove critical during the Hunger Games. Though Katniss doesn't feel spectacular, especially compared to some of the other tributes who are bigger and stronger than she is, she becomes one of the most notable among them, beginning with her appearance as "the girl who was on fire."

4. In District 12, we call them the Career Tributes, or just the Careers. And like as not, the winner will be one of them.

Katniss's explanation of what a Career Tribute is occurs when the tributes gather together for their first day of training in Chapter 7. As Katniss explains, the Career Tributes are those tributes from the wealthier districts (typically Districts 1, 2, and 4) who have trained their whole lives to take part in the Hunger Games. They know how to fight and use a variety of weapons, and they are typically large and look strong and well fed, compared to the tributes from the poorer districts, who often look undernourished. As a result, they are generally better prepared for the challenges of the Hunger Games and are typically the winners. When Katniss sees the other tributes for the first time on their first day of training, she realizes the Careers will pose the greatest threat to her survival in the arena.

In addition, the quote highlights the inequality between rich and poor in Panem, a major theme of the novel. Because of the tessera system, in which children eligible for the Hunger Games can have their names entered into the reaping additional times in exchange for extra rations of food, the poor are already more likely than the wealthy to be chosen as tributes. Since the poor are also ill-prepared for the Games when compared with the Career Tributes, they are at a serious disadvantage. Being chosen as a tribute is essentially a death sentence for the poor, whereas Career Tributes often volunteer to compete since winning for them is an honor rather than a matter of mere survival.

5. Peeta blushes beet red and stammers out, "Because... because...she came here with me."

In Chapter 9, as Caesar Flickerman interviews Peeta before the Games, Peeta reveals to Caesar and all of Panem that he's in love with Katniss. Peeta's revelation sets in motion the storyline of him and Katniss as ill-fated lovers that continues throughout the Games. This storyline has a significant influence on the Games and on Peeta and Katniss's survival. First, it makes Peeta and Katniss into a sensation among the viewers, in turn attracting sponsors. Haymitch has Katniss play up the romance for this reason, and in return he's able to secure gifts that prove vital, including food and the burn ointment Katniss uses to heal her leg. Second, the novel suggests that the love angle is the reason the Capitol decides to allow both tributes from a district to be named winners. The unprecedented move appears to be a response to Katniss and Peeta's popularity, and it is essentially the reason that both Katniss and Peeta survive the Hunger Games (though Katniss, of course, has to force the Capitol in the end).

Peeta's revelation of his love for Katniss is also the source of much of Katniss's internal conflict in the novel. Katniss can't discern whether Peeta is playing out a strategy devised by Haymitch or if his feelings are genuine. As a result, Katniss spends a great deal of time trying to puzzle out what Peeta really feels. When Peeta teams with the Careers, for instance, Katniss suspects he was lying and will do whatever is necessary to stay alive. Later he confuses Katniss by saving her at the expense of being injured himself, suggesting he really does care for her. She remains uncertain about Peeta's true feelings almost until the end of the novel, only conceding to herself that Peeta is telling the truth when he recalls details about the first time he saw her that prove he isn't simply acting.

6. And right now, the most dangerous part of the Hunger Games is about to begin.

Katniss says these words at the end of Chapter 26, after Haymitch tells her the Capitol was extremely angry at her stunt with the berries. The dangerous event Katniss refers to here is her interview with Caesar Flickerman, and it's dangerous because the lives of Katniss, her family, Peeta, and, even possibly, his family are now all at risk. As Haymitch told her, the Capitol feels that Katniss made them look foolish by forcing them to allow her and Peeta to both be declared winners after she and Peeta essentially threatened suicide. Consequently, though Katniss survived the Hunger Games, she is again in danger. She realizes that in her interview with Caesar

Flickerman she must convince everyone she suggested to Peeta they eat the poisonous berries because she couldn't bear the thought of losing him, not to deliberately defy the Capitol. In other words, she has to portray herself as desperately in love with Peeta and downplay any appearance of being a rebel. The quote and the events surrounding it again underscore how important appearances are in the novel.

Key Facts

FULL TITLE
The Hunger Games

AUTHOR
Suzanne Collins

TYPE OF WORK
Novel

GENRE
Dystopia

LANGUAGE
English

TIME AND PLACE WRITTEN
Connecticut, United States, in the early 2000s

DATE OF FIRST PUBLICATION
September 2008

PUBLISHER
Scholastic

NARRATOR
Katniss Everdeen narrates *The Hunger Games* as the events of the novel occur.

POINT OF VIEW
The story is told in the first person and recounts the narrator's personal history and experiences. The narrator is mostly objective, but on occasion she will imagine what other characters must be feeling.

TONE
Mostly stoic, but occasionally very emotional

TENSE
Present

SETTING (TIME)
An indeterminate time more than one hundred years in the future

SETTING (PLACE)

Panem, the country created after the governments of North America collapsed

PROTAGONIST

Katniss Everdeen

MAJOR CONFLICT

Katniss must endure numerous deadly ordeals, navigate complex personal relationships, and learn to control how others perceive her in order to survive the Hunger Games.

RISING ACTION

After volunteering to take her sister's place in the Hunger Games, Katniss has to manage others' perceptions of her to gain the best strategic advantage possible, then learn to survive inside the arena.

CLIMAX

Having outlasted the other tributes, Katniss and Peeta threaten suicide rather than fight one another after a rule change turns them from allies into adversaries.

FALLING ACTION

Even though she and Peeta won the Hunger Games, Katniss must try to assuage the Capitol, which is angry with her for threatening suicide and forcing a decision they didn't like.

THEMES

The inequality between rich and poor; suffering as entertainment; the importance of appearances

MOTIFS

Fire, defiance, hunting

SYMBOLS

Mockingjays, Panem, Katniss's dresses

FORESHADOWING

Katniss demonstrates her ability to hunt and forage in order to survive; Madge gives Katniss the mockingjay pin; Peeta excels at the camouflage station in training; Katniss saves the berries that killed Foxface.

Study Questions & Essay Topics

Study Questions

1. What role does debt play in the novel?

Debt, not of the financial sort necessarily but in the form of owing someone for their help, comes up multiple times in the novel. The most significant instance concerns Katniss's first encounter with Peeta. Katniss was starving at the time, and Peeta essentially saved her life by giving her bread from his family's bakery. Moreover, he apparently burned bread deliberately to help Katniss, despite knowing he would be punished as a result. Katniss describes how she has felt indebted to Peeta ever since. Thresh also brings up debt when he spares Katniss after learning about her alliance with Rue. He says they are "even," and no more is "owed."

These feelings of indebtedness, Katniss suggests, stem from the experience of growing up poor. When Peeta expresses his surprise that Thresh let Katniss live, Katniss tells him he wouldn't understand because he's "always had enough." What she implies is that Peeta has never been dependent on another person for either his or his loved ones' well-being, so he can't understand the feelings of debt associated with that experience. The tessera system plays into this mentality of indebtedness. The poor take extra food rations essentially on credit, which is paid back in the form of extra entries into the reaping. They often need the tessera in order to survive, so they take them knowing they will have to pay back what is essentially a debt later.

2. Does Katniss truly begin wanting a relationship with Peeta, or is she playing a role to gain a strategic advantage? Explain.

Though Katniss does begin to develop sincere romantic feelings for Peeta, she never appears to want their friendship to turn into a real relationship, and she keeps up the romance with Peeta primarily for the strategic advantage it provides. In numerous instances in which they kiss, Katniss thinks of what Haymitch would want to see rather than thinking that she actually wants to kiss Peeta, and only once does she say they shared a kiss that left her wanting another. In one of the most dramatic moments of their romance, Katniss tells Peeta he doesn't have competition anywhere, referring to Gale, but even in this situation she thinks of what Haymitch would want her to say.

Just as tellingly, when they're on their way back to District 12 Katniss makes it clear she doesn't think she's the type of person who can be in the sort of relationship Peeta wants. By all indications, she felt this way well before any romance began between them. Early in the novel, for instance, she thinks she could never get married and have children knowing that they might one day have to take part in the Hunger Games. Katniss's feelings, in other words, have not changed, and she is still not interested in a relationship, perhaps with anyone.

3. *Why does the author spend so much time focusing on the dresses Cinna creates for Katniss?*

Given that Katniss's life is at stake in the Hunger Games, the author's focus on Katniss's appearance at various times can seem frivolous. But as becomes clear over the course of the novel, appearances are extremely important to Katniss's survival. The author's focus on Cinna's dresses subtly emphasizes this theme by forcing the reader to take notice of Katniss's appearance. Katniss's dress for the opening ceremony, we learn, makes her (and Peeta, who is similarly dressed) stand apart from the other tributes. The significance of this move isn't fully clear until Katniss is in the arena and in need of sponsors. By making her stand out, the dress makes her popular, and this popularity is amplified by the public romance she shares with Peeta. Consequently, she becomes more likely to receive gifts, and these gifts actually turn out to be vital to her survival.

SUGGESTED ESSAY TOPICS

1. *Is Haymitch a good mentor to Katniss and Peeta? Explain.*

2. *In what ways does Katniss's hunting experience prepare her for the Games, and in what ways does it fail to prepare her?*

3. *How does Katniss's role in her family affect her behavior in the Games?*

4. *What is Katniss's greatest strength in the Games, and what is her greatest weakness?*

5. *Science fiction often uses a futuristic setting to comment on the present day. What does* THE HUNGER GAMES *suggest about the present-day United States?*

How to Write Literary Analysis

The Literary Essay: A Step-by-Step Guide

When you read for pleasure, your only goal is enjoyment. You might find yourself reading to get caught up in an exciting story, to learn about an interesting time or place, or just to pass time. Maybe you're looking for inspiration, guidance, or a reflection of your own life. There are as many different, valid ways of reading a book as there are books in the world.

When you read a work of literature in an English class, however, you're being asked to read in a special way: you're being asked to perform *literary analysis*. To analyze something means to break it down into smaller parts and then examine how those parts work, both individually and together. Literary analysis involves examining all the parts of a novel, play, short story, or poem—elements such as character, setting, tone, and imagery—and thinking about how the author uses those elements to create certain effects.

A literary essay isn't a book review: you're not being asked whether or not you liked a book or whether you'd recommend it to another reader. A literary essay also isn't like the kind of book report you wrote when you were younger, where your teacher wanted you to summarize the book's action. A high school or college-level literary essay asks, "How does this piece of literature actually work?" "How does it do what it does?" and, "Why might the author have made the choices he or she did?"

The Seven Steps

No one is born knowing how to analyze literature; it's a skill you learn and a process you can master. As you gain more practice with this kind of thinking and writing, you'll be able to craft a method that works best for you. But until then, here are seven basic steps to writing a well-constructed literary essay:

1. *Ask questions*
2. *Collect evidence*
3. *Construct a thesis*

4. Develop and organize arguments
5. Write the introduction
6. Write the body paragraphs
7. Write the conclusion

---

1. Ask Questions

When you're assigned a literary essay in class, your teacher will often provide you with a list of writing prompts. Lucky you! Now all you have to do is choose one. Do yourself a favor and pick a topic that interests you. You'll have a much better (not to mention easier) time if you start off with something you enjoy thinking about. If you are asked to come up with a topic by yourself, though, you might start to feel a little panicked. Maybe you have too many ideas—or none at all. Don't worry. Take a deep breath and start by asking yourself these questions:

- **What struck you?** Did a particular image, line, or scene linger in your mind for a long time? If it fascinated you, chances are you can draw on it to write a fascinating essay.
- **What confused you?** Maybe you were surprised to see a character act in a certain way, or maybe you didn't understand why the book ended the way it did. Confusing moments in a work of literature are like a loose thread in a sweater: if you pull on it, you can unravel the entire thing. Ask yourself why the author chose to write about that character or scene the way he or she did and you might tap into some important insights about the work as a whole.
- **Did you notice any patterns?** Is there a phrase that the main character uses constantly or an image that repeats throughout the book? If you can figure out how that pattern weaves through the work and what the significance of that pattern is, you've almost got your entire essay mapped out.
- **Did you notice any contradictions or ironies?** Great works of literature are complex; great literary essays recognize and explain those complexities. Maybe the title (*Happy Days*) totally disagrees with the book's subject matter (hungry orphans dying in the woods). Maybe the main character acts one way around his family and a completely different way around his friends and associates. If you can find a way to explain a work's contradictory elements, you've got the seeds of a great essay.

At this point, you don't need to know exactly what you're going to say about your topic; you just need a place to begin your exploration. You can help direct your reading and brainstorming by formulating your topic as a *question*, which you'll then try to answer in your essay. The best questions invite critical debates and discussions, not just a rehashing of the summary. Remember, you're looking for something you can *prove or argue* based on evidence you find in the text. Finally, remember to keep the scope of your question in mind: is this a topic you can adequately address within the word or page limit you've been given? Conversely, is this a topic big enough to fill the required length?

GOOD QUESTIONS

"Are Romeo and Juliet's parents responsible for the deaths of their children?"

"Why do pigs keep showing up in LORD OF THE FLIES*?"*

"Are Dr. Frankenstein and his monster alike? How?"

BAD QUESTIONS

"What happens to Scout in TO KILL A MOCKINGBIRD*?"*

"What do the other characters in JULIUS CAESAR *think about Caesar?"*

"How does Hester Prynne in THE SCARLET LETTER *remind me of my sister?"*

---

2. COLLECT EVIDENCE

Once you know what question you want to answer, it's time to scour the book for things that will help you answer the question. Don't worry if you don't know what you want to say yet—right now you're just collecting ideas and material and letting it all percolate. Keep track of passages, symbols, images, or scenes that deal with your topic. Eventually, you'll start making connections between these examples and your thesis will emerge.

Here's a brief summary of the various parts that compose each and every work of literature. These are the elements that you will analyze in your essay, and which you will offer as evidence to support your arguments.

ELEMENTS OF STORY These are the *whats* of the work—what happens, where it happens, and to whom it happens.

- **Plot:** All of the events and actions of the work.
- **Character:** The people who act and are acted upon in a literary work. The main character of a work is known as the *protagonist.*
- **Conflict:** The central tension in the work. In most cases, the protagonist wants something, while opposing forces (antagonists) hinder the protagonist's progress.
- **Setting:** When and where the work takes place. Elements of setting include location, time period, time of day, weather, social atmosphere, and economic conditions.
- **Narrator:** The person telling the story. The narrator may straightforwardly report what happens, convey the subjective opinions and perceptions of one or more characters, or provide commentary and opinion in his or her own voice.
- **Themes:** The main idea or message of the work—usually an abstract idea about people, society, or life in general. A work may have many themes, which may be in tension with one another.

ELEMENTS OF STYLE These are the *hows*—how the characters speak, how the story is constructed, and how language is used throughout the work.

- **Structure and organization:** How the parts of the work are assembled. Some novels are narrated in a linear, chronological fashion, while others skip around in time. Some plays follow a traditional three- or five-act structure, while others are a series of loosely connected scenes. Some authors deliberately leave gaps in their works, leaving readers to puzzle out the missing information. A work's structure and organization can tell you a lot about the kind of message it wants to convey.
- **Point of view:** The perspective from which a story is told. In *first-person point of view,* the narrator involves himself or herself in the story. ("I went to the store"; "We watched in horror as the bird slammed into the window.") A first-person narrator is usually the protagonist of the work, but not always. In *third-person point of view,* the narrator does not participate

in the story. A third-person narrator may closely follow a specific character, recounting that individual character's thoughts or experiences, or it may be what we call an *omniscient* narrator. Omniscient narrators see and know all: they can witness any event in any time or place and are privy to the inner thoughts and feelings of all characters. Remember that the narrator and the author are not the same thing!

- **Diction:** Word choice. Whether a character uses dry, clinical language or flowery prose with lots of exclamation points can tell you a lot about his or her attitude and personality.
- **Syntax:** Word order and sentence construction. Syntax is a crucial part of establishing an author's narrative voice. Ernest Hemingway, for example, is known for writing in very short, straightforward sentences, while James Joyce characteristically wrote in long, incredibly complicated lines.
- **Tone:** The mood or feeling of the text. Diction and syntax often contribute to the tone of a work. A novel written in short, clipped sentences that use small, simple words might feel brusque, cold, or matter-of-fact.
- **Imagery:** Language that appeals to the senses, representing things that can be seen, smelled, heard, tasted, or touched.
- **Figurative language:** Language that is not meant to be interpreted literally. The most common types of figurative language are *metaphors* and *similes,* which compare two unlike things in order to suggest a similarity between them—for example, "All the world's a stage," or "The moon is like a ball of green cheese." (Metaphors say one thing *is* another thing; similes claim that one thing is *like* another thing.)

---

3. CONSTRUCT A THESIS

When you've examined all the evidence you've collected and know how you want to answer the question, it's time to write your thesis statement. A *thesis* is a claim about a work of literature that needs to be supported by evidence and arguments. The thesis statement is the heart of the literary essay, and the bulk of your paper will be spent trying to prove this claim. A good thesis will be:

- **Arguable.** "*The Great Gatsby* describes New York society in the 1920s" isn't a thesis—it's a fact.

- **Provable through textual evidence.** "*Hamlet* is a confusing but ultimately very well-written play" is a weak thesis because it offers the writer's personal opinion about the book. Yes, it's arguable, but it's not a claim that can be proved or supported with examples taken from the play itself.
- **Surprising.** "Both George and Lenny change a great deal in *Of Mice and Men*" is a weak thesis because it's obvious. A really strong thesis will argue for a reading of the text that is not immediately apparent.
- **Specific.** "Dr. Frankenstein's monster tells us a lot about the human condition" is *almost* a really great thesis statement, but it's still too vague. What does the writer mean by "a lot"? *How* does the monster tell us so much about the human condition?

Good Thesis Statements

Question: In *Romeo and Juliet*, which is more powerful in shaping the lovers' story: fate or foolishness?

Thesis: "Though Shakespeare defines Romeo and Juliet as 'star-crossed lovers' and images of stars and planets appear throughout the play, a closer examination of that celestial imagery reveals that the stars are merely witnesses to the characters' foolish activities and not the causes themselves."

Question: How does the bell jar function as a symbol in Sylvia Plath's *The Bell Jar*?

Thesis: "A bell jar is a bell-shaped glass that has three basic uses: to hold a specimen for observation, to contain gases, and to maintain a vacuum. The bell jar appears in each of these capacities in *The Bell Jar*, Plath's semi-autobiographical novel, and each appearance marks a different stage in Esther's mental breakdown."

Question: Would Piggy in *The Lord of the Flies* make a good island leader if he were given the chance?

Thesis: "Though the intelligent, rational, and innovative Piggy has the mental characteristics of a good leader, he ultimately lacks the social skills necessary to be an effective one. Golding emphasizes this point by giving Piggy a foil in the charismatic Jack, whose magnetic personality allows him to capture and wield power effectively, if not always wisely."

4. Develop and Organize Arguments

The reasons and examples that support your thesis will form the middle paragraphs of your essay. Since you can't really write your thesis statement until you know how you'll structure your argument, you'll probably end up working on steps 3 and 4 at the same time.

There's no single method of argumentation that will work in every context. One essay prompt might ask you to compare and contrast two characters, while another asks you to trace an image through a given work of literature. These questions require different kinds of answers and therefore different kinds of arguments. Below, we'll discuss three common kinds of essay prompts and some strategies for constructing a solid, well-argued case.

Types of Literary Essays

- **Compare and contrast**

  Compare and contrast the characters of Huck and Jim in THE ADVENTURES OF HUCKLEBERRY FINN.

  Chances are you've written this kind of essay before. In an academic literary context, you'll organize your arguments the same way you would in any other class. You can either go *subject by subject* or *point by point*. In the former, you'll discuss one character first and then the second. In the latter, you'll choose several traits (attitude toward life, social status, images and metaphors associated with the character) and devote a paragraph to each. You may want to use a mix of these two approaches—for example, you may want to spend a paragraph apiece broadly sketching Huck's and Jim's personalities before transitioning into a paragraph or two describing a few key points of comparison. This can be a highly effective strategy if you want to make a counterintuitive argument—that, despite seeming to be totally different, the two characters being compared are actually similar in a very important way (or vice versa). Remember that your essay should reveal something fresh or unexpected about the text, so think beyond the obvious parallels and differences.

- **Trace**

  Choose an image—for example, birds, knives, or eyes—and trace that image throughout MACBETH.

  Sounds pretty easy, right? All you need to do is read the play, underline every appearance of a knife in *Macbeth*, and then list them in your essay in the order they appear, right? Well, not exactly. Your teacher doesn't want a simple catalog of examples. He or she wants to see you make *connections* between those examples—that's the difference between summarizing and analyzing. In the *Macbeth* example above, think about the different contexts in which knives appear in the play and to what effect. In *Macbeth*, there are real knives and imagined knives; knives that kill and knives that simply threaten. Categorize and classify your examples to give them some order. Finally, always keep the overall effect in mind. After you choose and analyze your examples, you should come to some greater understanding about the work, as well as your chosen image, symbol, or phrase's role in developing the major themes and stylistic strategies of that work.

- **Debate**

Is the society depicted in 1984 good for its citizens?

In this kind of essay, you're being asked to debate a moral, ethical, or aesthetic issue regarding the work. You might be asked to judge a character or group of characters (*Is Caesar responsible for his own demise?*) or the work itself (*Is* JANE EYRE *a feminist novel?*). For this kind of essay, there are two important points to keep in mind. First, don't simply base your arguments on your personal feelings and reactions. Every literary essay expects you to read and analyze the work, so search for evidence in the text. What do characters in *1984* have to say about the government of Oceania? What images does Orwell use that might give you a hint about his attitude toward the government? As in any debate, you also need to make sure that you define all the necessary terms before you begin to argue your case. What does it mean to be a "good" society? What makes a novel "feminist"? You should define your terms right up front, in the first paragraph after your introduction.

Second, remember that strong literary essays make contrary and surprising arguments. Try to think outside the box. In the *1984* example above, it seems like the obvious answer would be no, the totalitarian society depicted in Orwell's novel is *not* good for its citizens. But can you think of any arguments for the opposite side? Even if your final assertion is that the novel depicts a cruel, repressive, and therefore harmful society, acknowledging and responding to the counterargument will strengthen your overall case.

5. Write the Introduction

Your introduction sets up the entire essay. It's where you present your topic and articulate the particular issues and questions you'll be addressing. It's also where you, as the writer, introduce yourself to your readers. A persuasive literary essay immediately establishes its writer as a knowledgeable, authoritative figure.

An introduction can vary in length depending on the overall length of the essay, but in a traditional five-paragraph essay it should be no longer than one paragraph. However long it is, your introduction needs to:

- **Provide any necessary context.** Your introduction should situate the reader and let him or her know what to expect. What book are you discussing? Which characters? What topic will you be addressing?
- **Answer the "So what?" question.** Why is this topic important, and why is your particular position on the topic noteworthy? Ideally, your introduction should pique the reader's interest by suggesting how your argument is surprising or otherwise counterintuitive. Literary essays make unexpected connections and reveal less-than-obvious truths.
- **Present your thesis.** This usually happens at or very near the end of your introduction.
- **Indicate the shape of the essay to come.** Your reader should finish reading your introduction with a good sense of the scope of your essay as well as the path you'll take toward proving your thesis. You don't need to spell out every step, but you do need to suggest the organizational pattern you'll be using.

Your introduction should not:

- **Be vague.** Beware of the two killer words in literary analysis: *interesting* and *important*. Of course the work, question, or example is interesting and important—that's why you're writing about it!
- **Open with any grandiose assertions.** Many student readers think that beginning their essays with a flamboyant statement such as, "Since the dawn of time, writers have been fascinated with the topic of free will," makes them

sound important and commanding. You know what? It actually sounds pretty amateurish.

- **Wildly praise the work.** Another typical mistake student writers make is extolling the work or author. Your teacher doesn't need to be told that "Shakespeare is perhaps the greatest writer in the English language." You can mention a work's reputation in passing—by referring to *The Adventures of Huckleberry Finn* as "Mark Twain's enduring classic," for example—but don't make a point of bringing it up unless that reputation is key to your argument.
- **Go off-topic.** Keep your introduction streamlined and to the point. Don't feel the need to throw in all kinds of bells and whistles in order to impress your reader—just get to the point as quickly as you can, without skimping on any of the required steps.

---

6. WRITE THE BODY PARAGRAPHS

Once you've written your introduction, you'll take the arguments you developed in step 4 and turn them into your body paragraphs. The organization of this middle section of your essay will largely be determined by the argumentative strategy you use, but no matter how you arrange your thoughts, your body paragraphs need to do the following:

- **Begin with a strong topic sentence.** Topic sentences are like signs on a highway: they tell the reader where they are and where they're going. A good topic sentence not only alerts readers to what issue will be discussed in the following paragraph but also gives them a sense of what argument will be made *about* that issue. "Rumor and gossip play an important role in *The Crucible*" isn't a strong topic sentence because it doesn't tell us very much. "The community's constant gossiping creates an environment that allows false accusations to flourish" is a much stronger topic sentence—it not only tells us *what* the paragraph will discuss (gossip) but *how* the paragraph will discuss the topic (by showing how gossip creates a set of conditions that leads to the play's climactic action).
- **Fully and completely develop a single thought.** Don't skip around in your paragraph or try to stuff in too much material. Body paragraphs are like bricks: each individual

one needs to be strong and sturdy or the entire structure will collapse. Make sure you have really proven your point before moving on to the next one.

- **Use transitions effectively.** Good literary essay writers know that each paragraph must be clearly and strongly linked to the material around it. Think of each paragraph as a response to the one that precedes it. Use transition words and phrases such as *however, similarly, on the contrary, therefore,* and *furthermore* to indicate what kind of response you're making.

---

7. WRITE THE CONCLUSION

Just as you used the introduction to ground your readers in the topic before providing your thesis, you'll use the conclusion to quickly summarize the specifics learned thus far and then hint at the broader implications of your topic. A good conclusion will:

- **Do more than simply restate the thesis.** If your thesis argued that *The Catcher in the Rye* can be read as a Christian allegory, don't simply end your essay by saying, "And that is why *The Catcher in the Rye* can be read as a Christian allegory." If you've constructed your arguments well, this kind of statement will just be redundant.
- **Synthesize the arguments, not summarize them.** Similarly, don't repeat the details of your body paragraphs in your conclusion. The reader has already read your essay, and chances are it's not so long that they've forgotten all your points by now.
- **Revisit the "So what?" question.** In your introduction, you made a case for why your topic and position are important. You should close your essay with the same sort of gesture. What do your readers know now that they didn't know before? How will that knowledge help them better appreciate or understand the work overall?
- **Move from the specific to the general.** Your essay has most likely treated a very specific element of the work—a single character, a small set of images, or a particular passage. In your conclusion, try to show how this narrow discussion has wider implications for the work overall. If your essay on *To Kill a Mockingbird* focused on the character of Boo Radley, for example, you might want to include a bit in your

conclusion about how he fits into the novel's larger message about childhood, innocence, or family life.

- **Stay relevant.** Your conclusion should suggest new directions of thought, but it shouldn't be treated as an opportunity to pad your essay with all the extra, interesting ideas you came up with during your brainstorming sessions but couldn't fit into the essay proper. Don't attempt to stuff in unrelated queries or too many abstract thoughts.
- **Avoid making overblown closing statements.** A conclusion should open up your highly specific, focused discussion, but it should do so without drawing a sweeping lesson about life or human nature. Making such observations may be part of the point of reading, but it's almost always a mistake in essays, where these observations tend to sound overly dramatic or simply silly.

A+ Essay Checklist

Congratulations! If you've followed all the steps we've outlined above, you should have a solid literary essay to show for all your efforts. What if you've got your sights set on an A+? To write the kind of superlative essay that will be rewarded with a perfect grade, keep the following rubric in mind. These are the qualities that teachers expect to see in a truly A+ essay. How does yours stack up?

- ✓ Demonstrates a thorough understanding of the book
- ✓ Presents an original, compelling argument
- ✓ Thoughtfully analyzes the text's formal elements
- ✓ Uses appropriate and insightful examples
- ✓ Structures ideas in a logical and progressive order
- ✓ Demonstrates a mastery of sentence construction, transitions, grammar, spelling, and word choice

A+ STUDENT ESSAY

How do appearances differ from reality in the novel? How does each side—the Capitol being one and the citizens in the districts being the other—use appearances to their advantage?

Honesty is always among the first victims of any dictatorship. Leaving no room for dissent doesn't mean it disappears, just that it goes into hiding. In the novel, Capitol-controlled Panem is no exception. The Capitol is afraid of any deviation from its official line, because a deviation, especially a public one, threatens its control. The people, meanwhile, fear punishment by the government, and so they fall in step and march to the government's drum, at least outwardly. All the fear creates an outward facade, one in which the Capitol and its citizens are in perfect harmony. The reality, however, is quite different. Beneath that facade is a seething mass of dissent, and the great irony in *The Hunger Games* is that everyone knows it. The appearance of unity and conformity is just a fiction, one that both sides, for very different reasons, have a stake in preserving.

As a consequence, appearances become something of a weapon, which the Capitol and the people of Panem each try to use to their advantage. The Capitol, for instance, enforces the illusion of widespread conformity as a way to hide dissent and maintain control. It demands that people in the districts regard the annual Hunger Games as an event to be celebrated, even though for them it means sacrificing two local children. There are televised interviews with the tributes and grand events like the opening ceremony, where the tributes appear in elaborate costumes. Forcing everyone to participate and act as if they like the Games means that anyone bold enough to dissent openly will stand out, making them easy to target. People who don't publicly rebel against the Capitol can of course remain hidden, but it means they remain hidden from each other as well. It's much harder for rebels to find one another and organize if they can't spot each other. Maintaining the appearance of monolithic support for the Games across the districts thus acts as an effective way to suppress potential opposition.

This principle cuts both ways, however. If rebels can't spot other rebels because they're all conforming to hide their real feelings, it's also harder for the Capitol to spot them. People like Katniss take advantage of this invisibility and use it. Katniss appears outwardly to be a normal teenager like any other in District 12; by not calling attention to herself, she's able to hunt illegally to feed her family.

The power of appearances is amplified in the context of the Hunger Games. Again, the Capitol forces people to be complicit in an illusion, but this time it's the tributes. They act as if it's an honor to take part in the Games, and for the career tributes—those who have trained their whole lives in anticipation of competing in the Games—it may be so. But for the majority it's essentially a death sentence. The Capitol needs the tributes to maintain the fiction that they're willing contestants, though, because otherwise the Games become horrific and cease to be entertainment. They would be revealed for what they actually are, the state-sanctioned murder of children. It's a sly bit of marketing that allows the Capitol to act as if the tributes aren't really victims.

The tributes are also able to use appearances to their advantage, however, with Katniss doing so in the most significant way. The Games are recorded and broadcast, so what the viewers at home see is, for the most part, what the tributes want them to see; playing to the cameras helps the tributes win gifts, which can literally mean the difference between life and death. It becomes an integral part of Haymitch's and Katniss's strategy. Haymitch manages to communicate to Katniss that he wants her to pretend to be in love with Peeta for this reason, and the ploy works extremely well. Their romance becomes so popular among the viewers at home that Katniss and Peeta begin receiving valuable gifts, and a rule change stating that two tributes from the same district can win the Games is announced. Katniss ultimately uses the story that they're in love to force the Capitol to allow both of them to live, because once all the other tributes have died, the Capitol announces that they're reverting to the original rules and allowing only one winner. Katniss and Peeta threaten to commit suicide with poisonous berries, and the Capitol, knowing that such an outcome would look extremely bad for them, backs down. It's essentially the power of appearances that allows Katniss to keep herself and Peeta alive.

That these superficial facades carry so much influence reveals the delicate balance that exists in Panem. If appearances shift too much in any direction, either revealing the Capitol to be a brutal dictatorship or showing that the people in the districts can defy the Capitol with impunity, that balance could collapse. At the end of the novel, Katniss discovers that her threat of suicide with Peeta may, in fact, have thrown off that balance, since many see it as a gesture of open defiance. Even just the appearance of rebellion, the Capitol fears, has the power to upend the entire system.

GLOSSARY OF LITERARY TERMS

ANTAGONIST
The entity that acts to frustrate the goals of the *protagonist.* The antagonist is usually another *character* but may also be a non-human force.

ANTIHERO / ANTIHEROINE
A *protagonist* who is not admirable or who challenges notions of what should be considered admirable.

CHARACTER
A person, animal, or any other thing with a personality that appears in a *narrative.*

CLIMAX
The moment of greatest intensity in a text or the major turning point in the *plot.*

CONFLICT
The central struggle that moves the *plot* forward. The conflict can be the *protagonist*'s struggle against fate, nature, society, or another person.

FIRST-PERSON POINT OF VIEW
A literary style in which the *narrator* tells the story from his or her own *point of view* and refers to himself or herself as "I." The narrator may be an active participant in the story or just an observer.

HERO / HEROINE
The principal *character* in a literary work or *narrative.*

IMAGERY
Language that brings to mind sense-impressions, representing things that can be seen, smelled, heard, tasted, or touched.

MOTIF
A recurring idea, structure, contrast, or device that develops or informs the major *themes* of a work of literature.

NARRATIVE
A story.

NARRATOR

The person (sometimes a *character*) who tells a story; the *voice* assumed by the writer. The narrator and the author of the work of literature are not the same person.

PLOT

The arrangement of the events in a story, including the sequence in which they are told, the relative emphasis they are given, and the causal connections between events.

POINT OF VIEW

The *perspective* that a *narrative* takes toward the events it describes.

PROTAGONIST

The main *character* around whom the story revolves.

SETTING

The location of a *narrative* in time and space. Setting creates mood or atmosphere.

SUBPLOT

A secondary *plot* that is of less importance to the overall story but may serve as a point of contrast or comparison to the main plot.

SYMBOL

An object, *character,* figure, or color that is used to represent an abstract idea or concept. Unlike an *emblem,* a symbol may have different meanings in different contexts.

SYNTAX

The way the words in a piece of writing are put together to form lines, phrases, or clauses; the basic structure of a piece of writing.

THEME

A fundamental and universal idea explored in a literary work.

TONE

The author's attitude toward the subject or *characters* of a story or poem or toward the reader.

VOICE

An author's individual way of using language to reflect his or her own personality and attitudes. An author communicates voice through *tone, diction,* and *syntax.*

A NOTE ON PLAGIARISM

Plagiarism—presenting someone else's work as your own—rears its ugly head in many forms. Many students know that copying text without citing it is unacceptable. But some don't realize that even if you're not quoting directly, but instead are paraphrasing or summarizing, *it is plagiarism* unless you cite the source.

Here are the most common forms of plagiarism:

- Using an author's phrases, sentences, or paragraphs without citing the source
- Paraphrasing an author's ideas without citing the source
- Passing off another student's work as your own

How do you steer clear of plagiarism? You should *always* acknowledge all words and ideas that aren't your own by using quotation marks around verbatim text or citations like footnotes and endnotes to note another writer's ideas. For more information on how to give credit when credit is due, ask your teacher for guidance or visit www.sparknotes.com.

Review & Resources

Quiz

1. What is Katniss's sister's full first name?

   A. Pamela
   B. Primly
   C. Prim
   D. Primrose

2. How did Katniss's father die?

   A. In a hunting accident
   B. In a mine explosion
   C. He became trapped in a collapsed mine
   D. He was murdered by the Capitol

3. At what skill is Gale better than Katniss?

   A. Setting snares
   B. Using an axe
   C. Swimming
   D. Bird calls

4. Who or what is Katniss named after?

   A. Her grandmother
   B. A plant with edible roots
   C. A type of bird
   D. Catnip

5. Who gives Katniss the mockingjay pin?

   A. Gale
   B. Cinna
   C. Madge
   D. Prim

6. Why does the Capitol hold the Hunger Games?

   A. As a way to control the size of the population
   B. To keep the districts happy
   C. Because they are part of a religious festival
   D. To remind the districts that they are powerless against it

7. Which word best describes Haymitch?

   A. Sensitive
   B. Polite
   C. Silly
   D. Gruff

8. Under what circumstances did Katniss first meet Peeta?

   A. Katniss was looking for food and Peeta gave her bread
   B. They were both in the woods hunting
   C. They did a project at school together
   D. Peeta was injured and Katniss's mother helped him

9. What does Katniss think when she first sees the residents of the Capitol?

   A. They are sophisticated and beautiful
   B. They are superficial and ridiculous
   C. They are overweight and tall
   D. They are ungroomed and slovenly

10. What are tesserae?

   A. Extra rations of grain and oil
   B. Hybrid animals created by the Capitol
   C. A type of plant
   D. What the children are called who are chosen to compete in the Games

11. Which training station does Peeta excel at?

   A. Archery
   B. Knife throwing
   C. Camouflage
   D. Knot tying

12. What does Peeta tell Katniss he wants to do in the Games?

A. Kill as many Career Tributes as possible
B. Hide
C. Find a way to escape the arena
D. Show the Capitol he's not just a piece in their game

13. What item does Katniss manage to grab at the Cornucopia when the Games begin?

A. Bow
B. Knife
C. Backpack
D. Helmet

14. What is the first thing Katniss looks for after running from the Cornucopia?

A. Food
B. Water
C. Shelter
D. Fire

15. What does Peeta do that surprises Katniss on their first night in the arena?

A. He hunts with the Career Tributes
B. He camouflages himself expertly in mud
C. He kisses Katniss
D. He cries

16. When Katniss is severely dehydrated, how does Haymitch indicate to her that she's near water?

A. He sends her a map
B. He sends her a cup
C. He sends her iodine drops
D. He doesn't send her anything

17. What does Rue point out to Katniss that lets her get away from the group of Career Tributes?

A. A sheaf of arrows
B. A tracker jacker nest
C. A boulder
D. A mockinjay nest

18. What do Rue and Katniss realize is their advantage over the Career Tributes?

A. They can hide well
B. They're faster
C. They can hunt and forage their own food
D. They're deadlier with weapons

19. What does Katniss do when Rue is killed?

A. She buries her body
B. She camouflages her body
C. She covers her body in flowers
D. She runs away as fast as she can

20. Where does Katniss find Peeta after it's declared that two tributes can win the Games?

A. Hiding in a cave
B. Lying camouflaged in mud
C. In a tree
D. By the Cornucopia

21. How does Haymitch indicate to Katniss that he wants her to play up the romance with Peeta?

A. He sends her a pot of broth after she and Peeta kiss
B. He sends her a note telling her what he wants her to do
C. He sends her an item from Gale
D. He doesn't send her anything

22. What does Thresh say to Katniss when he spares her life?

A. He can't kill a girl
B. He's in love with her
C. He's afraid of her
D. They're even now

23. How does Cato finally die?

A. The muttations kill him
B. Katniss shoots him
C. He eats poisonous berries
D. He starves to death

24. How do Katniss and Peeta force the Capitol to declare them both winners?

A. They threaten to run away
B. They threaten that the winner will tell about everything
C. They threaten to commit suicide
D. They threaten to cause a rebellion against the Capitol

25. What event does Katniss refer to when she says the most dangerous part of the Hunger Games is about to begin?

A. Her last interview with Caesar Flickerman
B. Her imminent confrontation with Cato at the Cornucopia
C. Her entrance into the arena
D. Her first kiss with Peeta

ANSWER KEY

1. D; 2. B; 3. A; 4. B; 5. C; 6. D; 7. D; 8. A; 9. B; 10. A; 11. C; 12. D; 13. C; 14. B; 15. A; 16. D; 17. B; 18. C; 19. C; 20. B; 21. A; 22. D; 23. B; 24. C; 25. A

SUGGESTIONS FOR FURTHER READING

CARPENTER, CAROLINE. *Guide to the Hunger Games.* New Jersey: Plexus Publishing, 2012.

DOMINUS, SUSAN. "Suzanne Collins's War Stories for Kids." *The New York Times*, April 8, 2011.

FRANKEL, VALERIE ESTELLE. *Katniss the Cattail: An Unauthorized Guide to Names and Symbols in Suzanne Collins' The Hunger Games.* CreateSpace, 2012.

GRESH, LOIS H. *The Hunger Games Companion: The Unauthorized Guide to the Series.* New York: St. Martin's Griffin, 2011.

POLLITT, KATHA. "The Hunger Games' Feral Feminism." *The Nation*, April 3, 2012.

SEIFE, EMILY. *The Hunger Games Tribute Guide.* New York: Scholastic Press, 2012.

King Minos lived on Crete.

He had a Strong Navy and would often invade Athens the capital city of Greece. The King of Athens begged for the invasions to stop. So King Minos said, "well I have this Minator that needs to be fed." Send me seven boys and girls as tribute every year.

p.153 Katniss eats bark.

L3 create characters

L4 -> small group scenarios

L5 -> writing a scripts / reading a different scenario

L6 -> revisions

L7 -> Staged readings.

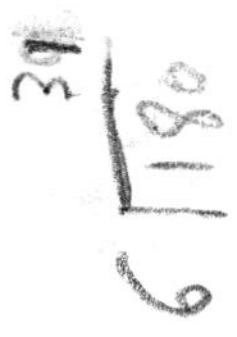

SparkNotes Literature Guides

1984
The Adventures of Huckleberry Finn
The Adventures of Tom Sawyer
The Alchemist
The Aeneid
All Quiet on the Western Front
And Then There Were None
Angela's Ashes
Animal Farm
Anna Karenina
Anne of Green Gables
Anthem
Antony and Cleopatra
Aristotle's Ethics
As I Lay Dying
As You Like It
Atlas Shrugged
The Autobiography of Malcolm X
The Awakening
The Bean Trees
The Bell Jar
Beloved
Beowulf
Billy Budd
Black Boy
Bless Me, Ultima
The Bluest Eye
Brave New World
The Brothers Karamazov
The Call of the Wild
Candide
The Canterbury Tales
Catch-22
The Catcher in the Rye
The Chocolate War
The Chosen
Cold Mountain
Cold Sassy Tree
The Color Purple
The Count of Monte Cristo
Crime and Punishment
The Crucible
Cry, the Beloved Country
The Curious Incident of the Dog in the Night-Time
Cyrano de Bergerac
David Copperfield
Death of a Salesman
The Death of Socrates
The Diary of a Young Girl
A Doll's House
Don Quixote
Dr. Faustus
Dr. Jekyll and Mr. Hyde
Dracula
Dune
Mythology
Emma
Ethan Frome
Fahrenheit 451
Fallen Angels
A Farewell to Arms
Farewell to Manzanar
Flowers for Algernon
For Whom the Bell Tolls
The Fountainhead
Frankenstein
The Giver
The Glass Menagerie
Gone With the Wind
The Good Earth
The Grapes of Wrath
Great Expectations
The Great Gatsby
Grendel
Gulliver's Travels
Hamlet
The Handmaid's Tale
Hard Times
Harry Potter and the Sorcerer's Stone
Heart of Darkness
Henry IV, Part I
Henry V
Hiroshima
The Hobbit
The House of Seven Gables
The Hunger Games
I Know Why the Caged Bird Sings
The Iliad
Inferno
Inherit the Wind
Invisible Man
Jane Eyre
Johnny Tremain
The Joy Luck Club
Julius Caesar
The Jungle
The Killer Angels
The Kite Runner
King Lear
The Last of the Mohicans
Les Misérables
A Lesson Before Dying
The Little Prince
Little Women
Lord of the Flies
The Lord of the Rings
Macbeth
Madame Bovary
A Man for All Seasons
The Mayor of Casterbridge
The Merchant of Venice
A Midsummer Night's Dream
Moby-Dick
Much Ado About Nothing
My Antonia
Narrative of the Life of Frederick Douglass
Native Son
The New Testament
Night
Notes from Underground
The Odyssey
The Oedipus Plays
Of Mice and Men
The Old Man and the Sea
The Old Testament
Oliver Twist
The Once and Future King
One Day in the Life of Ivan Denisovich
One Flew Over the Cuckoo's Nest
One Hundred Years of Solitude
Othello
Our Town
The Outsiders
Paradise Lost
A Passage to India
The Pearl
The Picture of Dorian Gray
Poe's Short Stories
A Portrait of the Artist as a Young Man
Pride and Prejudice
The Prince
A Raisin in the Sun
The Red Badge of Courage
The Republic
Richard III
Robinson Crusoe
Romeo and Juliet
The Scarlet Letter
A Separate Peace
Silas Marner
Sir Gawain and the Green Knight
Slaughterhouse-Five
Snow Falling on Cedars
Song of Solomon
The Sound and the Fury
Steppenwolf
The Stranger
A Streetcar Named Desire
The Sun Also Rises
A Tale of Two Cities
The Taming of the Shrew
The Tempest
Tess of the d'Urbevilles
The Things They Carried
Their Eyes Were Watching God
Things Fall Apart
To Kill a Mockingbird
To the Lighthouse
Treasure Island
Twelfth Night
Ulysses
Uncle Tom's Cabin
Walden
War and Peace
Wuthering Heights
A Yellow Raft in Blue Water